HAPPY

THIS

YEAR!

THE SECRET TO GETTING HAPPY
ONCE AND FOR ALL

HAPPY  THIS YEAR!

THE SECRET TO GETTING HAPPY ONCE AND FOR ALL

Will Bowen

GRAND
HARBOR
PRESS

Published by Brilliance Publishing

1704 Eaton Drive

Grand Haven, MI 49417

ISBN-13: 9781611099294

ISBN-10: 1611099293

Library of Congress Control Number: 2012951303

DEDICATION

*For my dad, Bill, whose example
keeps me on my path.*

ACKNOWLEDGMENTS

Thank you to Grand Harbor Press for affording me the great honor of being the first author in its new religion and spirituality imprint—I look forward to many years working together to help inspire and awaken human consciousness. Gary Krebs, your insights and guidance have been invaluable. Steve Hanselman of LevelFiveMedia, my literary agent and friend, you continue to be an invaluable resource, sounding board, and mentor. Thank you to Julia Serebrinsky for your patience in helping me refine my ideas and clarify my direction. Marti Lee, your happy example first inspired me to attempt to fully awaken happiness within myself. Thank you to my daughter, Lia, for your support and insights that far exceed your years. Thanks to all of my spiritual partners at InVision; your belief in me and support of my work brings me more joy than you will ever know. Terry Lund, your prayers have helped me maintain the highest perspective for my life. Thank you to Reed and Anita Brown for sharing your home, your hearts, and your culture with me; blessings to you and to "all my relatives." And thank you to Clay Johnston and Robin Kowalski for helping me take a fresh look at raising people's happiness levels.

Contents

INTRODUCTION

Happiness lies in the consciousness we have of it, and by no means in the way the future keeps its promises.
—George Sand

Your destiny is to be happy.

Deep within your heart, you know this to be true. The underlying reason for everything human beings aspire to do, achieve, or possess is sourced by an unstated and often unconscious belief that it will somehow increase their overall level of happiness. And yet high and enduring levels of happiness tend to find ways of eluding us.

You can become measurably and sustainably happier this year. This book will inspire you to draw a line in the sands of your life and declare unequivocally that over the next 12 months you will begin to experience a happier life. At this pronouncement, you may feel a surge of giddy excitement—as well as a pang of nagging doubt—but within these pages, you will find both the processes and shifts necessary to enjoy increased levels of happiness.

Becoming happier takes effort, but what you probably don't realize is that you are already expending a great deal of effort trying to be happy and yet are probably not fully realizing the results you seek.

In this book, you will discover new ways to bring forth higher levels of happiness and, more important, you will learn how to let go of things that you've been doing that are actually impeding your progress.

You will notice that I will often compare the process of becoming a happier person to becoming more physically fit. This is a relatable metaphor, and you will find that the two major elements to achieving increased fitness are the same for becoming a happier person.

The two components that determine your level of fitness—nutrition (what you put into your body) and exercise (what you do with your body)—are the same for being happy. What you put into your mind and what you do with your mind strengthen your emotional state, allowing you to enjoy higher and higher levels of happiness.

A TRULY HAPPY NEW YEAR!

We will consider the transformation to a happier life within the context of a New Year, but don't get caught up in this metaphor. Whether this book enters your hands and begins to merge with your consciousness on January 1, February 10, July 14, or whatever day, it marks the beginning of a New Year for you and a happier new life.

The advent of a New Year is inextricably linked to happiness the world over, as you can see in the following examples:

- In the United States, as well as in many other countries, the New Year is celebrated with "Happy New Year!" exclamations.

- In China, people display the *fú* characters—which stand for "blessings" or "happiness"—in their homes at the beginning of each New Year. And, prior to receiving traditional red envelopes containing money, Chinese children wish their parents a "healthy and happy New Year."

- In Japan, New Year's celebrations traditionally include the serving of *kohaku kamaboko*, red and white fish cakes—the red color symbolizing happiness.

- On New Year's Eve, Mexicans court happiness by wearing colorful underwear.

- Similarly, precisely at midnight on New Year's Eve, Brazilians rush to don yellow underwear, believing that this will produce greater happiness in the coming year.

- As part of their New Year celebrations, Ecuadorians burn pictures of unhappy moments from the previous year as a means of purging negativity and opening themselves up to happier experiences in the coming year.

- Citizens of Turkey welcome the New Year by engaging in philanthropic activity, believing that doing good deeds for others will bring greater happiness in the coming 12 months.

Not only do New Year's rituals around the globe center around happiness but it is also our universal desire to experience happiness that causes people the world over to engage in setting New Year's resolutions. Deep down we believe, although we rarely acknowledge it, that setting intentions to make positive changes in our behaviors and habits during the coming year will ultimately bring about increased happiness.

According to *USA.gov*, a US government website, the most common New Year's resolutions in the United States are:

- Drink less alcohol.
- Eat healthy food.
- Get a better education.
- Get a better job.
- Get fit.
- Lose weight.
- Manage debt.
- Manage stress.
- Quit smoking.
- Reduce, reuse, and recycle.
- Save money.
- Take a trip.
- Volunteer to help others

Did you notice that "become happier" isn't on the list? That's because becoming happier is the unmentioned desired result of all of our resolutions.

Ask yourself, why do people make resolutions such as those listed above? For example, why would someone resolve to drink less alcohol? Reasons vary by the individual, but perhaps the answer might be to become clearer in mind and healthier in body.

The question then becomes, "Why would someone aspire to have a clearer mind and a healthier body?"

Answer: To feel better and to enjoy life more.

To enjoy life more = to be happier.

Let's consider another example from the *USA.gov* list: to reduce, reuse, and recycle.

Why would a person wish to lessen his or her environmental imprint by reducing consumption, reusing what can be reused, and recycling what can't? Again, individual motives vary, but perhaps it is to feel a sense of making the world a better place; to feel as if he or she is making a difference—in short, to feel good.

To feel good = to be happy.

If we dig deeply enough, all New Year's resolutions circle back to a longing for increased happiness.

It's been joked that New Year's resolutions are a to-do list for the first week in January. Most New Year's resolutions, however well intentioned, scatter like birds shortly after they are made only to reappear the following year.

As each successive New Year arrives, we eagerly aspire to improve our health, relationships, finances, and careers in the unrealized belief that this will ultimately raise our level of happiness. Sadly, as the years of our lives pass, too many of us only see our good intentions collapsing upon a trail of relapses and our highest aspirations stalling into spinouts, creating a growing sense that change is too hard and that we ought to just accept our lot in life.

THE FIRST STEP TOWARD HAPPINESS

The problem with resolutions for change is that they are often formed from the unstated and unreal belief that we are overcoming a personal deficiency in order to reach a happier state.

This focus is like looking the wrong way through a telescope—at effects, rather than causes. In reality, we must first understand that happiness is a karmic process that moves from causes in our thoughts, speech, and actions, and ultimately imprints itself upon our habits, our character, and our destiny. When we understand the nature of this process and learn to properly align our practices within it, we can begin to actually improve ourselves with an eye toward enhanced growth rather than a false focus on overcoming a deficiency.

Happiness is an internal process. We often seek changes in the outer world, thinking it will impact our sense of well-being, when in reality, studies have found that it's the other way around. As you'll learn in Chapter 6, becoming a happier person positively impacts our health, relationships, finances, careers, and much more. Ever-increasing levels of happiness can be maintained every day with proper mental nutrition and exercise. Regardless of what the year and your life may bring, you *can* become a happy person.

The first step to happiness is to embrace the truth that you are *already happy*. Happiness is like fitness. People say they want to be fit, when in actuality everyone is *already* fit to some extent. Likewise, everyone is *already* somewhat happy. Both happiness and fitness levels exist along a continuum.

We can set fitness goals and measure improvement by weighing ourselves, checking our body fat percentage, measuring our ability to perform certain physical exercises, calculating our flexibility, and other benchmarks.

However, unlike fitness, a person's level of happiness is subjective. In fact, many scientists prefer the term "subjective well-being" to "happiness."

RAISING YOUR HAPPYSTAT

Although many researchers are attempting to quantify happiness, such efforts have, thus far, proven inconclusive. Economist Deirdre N. McCloskey explains the inherent subjectivity in measuring happiness in her June 8, 2012, article "Happyism," published in the *New Republic*. Likening our perception of happiness to our perception of color, she writes, "We cannot ever know whether your experience of the color red is the same as mine, no matter how many brain scans we take." Similarly, one person's level of happiness is never the quite same as another's.

Your happiness level is not only subjective, it is also less attached to your life experiences than you may think.

The year prior to my writing this manuscript was a difficult one for me. In addition to my mother passing away, I experienced a number of other significant challenges and setbacks, which I'll touch on in Chapter 5.

One evening, as I prepared to go to bed, I realized that I had been quite happy throughout that day. This seemed odd, considering all that had recently transpired in my life, and I wondered aloud, "On a scale of one to ten, how happy was I today?" I reasoned that I had been about an 8.5. Taking a marker designed to write on glass I wrote on my bathroom mirror: "Happiness Level: 8.5" and the date.

The following morning, I looked at my mirror and saw the evaluation of my happiness level from yesterday. I set an intention to do my best to maintain that same level throughout the coming day, regardless of what transpired. That evening, I honestly felt I had averaged another happiness level of 8.5 and once again I noted this on the mirror.

I repeated my little experiment every day for two weeks and found that even with the vagaries and challenges of life, I was able to maintain between an 8 and 10 each day. In this experience, I discovered the truth of Abraham Lincoln's words: "Folks are usually about as happy as they make up their minds to be."

STAKING YOUR CLAIM TO HAPPINESS

Before we even begin, determine how happy you feel you are and decide—yes, *decide*—how happy you wish to become as a result of applying what you will learn in this book.

Make your self-selected happiness level your all-consuming, all-year-round New Year's resolution. Once you increase your level of happiness, there will be plenty of time to lose weight, quit smoking, find true love, or any of the other typical New Year's resolutions we so often make and yet so rarely accomplish.

In Matthew 6:33, Jesus of Nazareth is quoted to have said, "Seek ye first the kingdom of God, and his righteousness; and all these things shall be added unto you." Regardless of your religious leanings, you know that what Jesus referred to as the "Kingdom of God" or, as many would call it, "heaven," must certainly be a place where happiness reigns supreme.

In Luke 17:21, Jesus tells us exactly where this happy place is to be found. He says, "The kingdom of God is within you."

Within you exists a higher level of happiness. Together we are going to call it forth.

WHAT IS HAPPINESS?

In Lewis Carroll's classic children's story *Alice's Adventures in Wonderland*, Alice has the following exchange with the Cheshire Cat:

Alice: Would you tell me, please, which way to go from here?
Cheshire Cat: That depends a good deal
on where you want to get to.

Before we can consider which way to go from where we are, we must agree on where we want to end up. If our desire is to become happy, then let's begin by having a realistic understanding of what it means to be happy.

There are a lot of suppositions and misunderstandings as to what happiness is.

Over the last several years, I have read many books on happiness and studied happiness from different angles. The best definition for happiness I found was summarized in a January 2009 *Psychology Today* article:

> *What is happiness? The most useful definition—and it's one agreed upon by neuroscientists, psychiatrists, behavioral economists, positive psychologists, and Buddhist monks—is more like satisfied or content than "happy" in its strict bursting-with-glee sense.*

Glee, bliss, elation, jubilation, and joy are the great symphonic crescendos of life. As magnificent as they are—and we should seek them out and enjoy them to their fullest—it is not realistic to think we can live in a state of never-ending euphoria

Happiness is a sense of contentment and well-being that pervades our lives, whereas joy is a firework that explodes brilliantly and fades quickly.

The Catcher in the Rye author J. D. Salinger expressed the difference between happiness and joy perfectly. In his short story "De Daumier-Smith's Blue Period," Salinger wrote, "The most singular difference between happiness and joy is that happiness is a solid and joy a liquid."

Happiness is the beach. Joy is the waves. Happiness is an emotional foundation of our lives, whereas joy ebbs and flows and is dependent on what occurs in our lives.

Many psychologists believe that we have a happiness "set point"—a level of happiness that we return to, regardless of what transpires in our day-to-day lives.

By way of example, let's suppose our happiness set point tends to hover around a 6.5 on a 10-point scale. When something wonderful happens—such as being asked out on a date by someone we are attracted to, getting a great new job, or discovering a wonderful new restaurant—we get a burst of joy. However, after the initial bump, we tend to settle back down to our predominant happiness level.

This happiness set point concept works both ways. Some researchers have found that after a traumatic event most people's level of happiness will dip proportionate to the experience, but will tend to rise over time back to the typical level.

When it comes to rebounding from negative experiences, this is comforting. However, most of us would agree that it would be nice to stay at a higher level after a positive experience.

The purpose of this book is to help you raise your happiness set point so that as life's ups and downs occur, you settle back to ever-higher levels.

YOUR EMOTIONAL GOVERNOR

When I was 13, my older brother Chuck drove a school bus. He was only 17 at the time, and the school officials knew all too well the tendency of teenage boys to drive too fast. In an effort to ensure the safety of the students who rode the buses, the school district fitted the engines of each bus with a governor device that capped the vehicle's maximum speed. This meant that while the school buses were capable of going 70 miles per hour or faster, the governor would prevent them from exceeding 45 mph.

The Governor on the Bus Is Like Your Emotional Governor

On level roads—regardless of the speed limit—the bus could not exceed 45 mph.

This is akin to your predominant happiness level. You tend to stay at an average level that is typical for you when life is going along smoothly.

When the school bus went up a steep hill, its weight and the grade of the incline would keep it from reaching even its 45 mph governed maximum speed.

When things get tough in life, you may average well below your happiness set point. Fortunately, however, school buses don't always drive uphill and your life is not always challenging.

Once the school bus crested the hill and began to come down the other side, gravity added to its speed and, even though the engine's governor was supposed to prevent it from going faster than 45 mph, the bus might reach 60 or 70 mph. Soon, however, it would either reach level ground and its speed would sink back to 45 mph.

Whether you know it or not, you have an emotional governor—a happiness set point. It keeps you from maintaining higher sustained levels of happiness, although you might experience fleeting moments of joy. If we were to attempt to find your happiness governor we could not because, unlike the mechanical one affixed to the school bus, yours dwells in the depths of your mind.

Together, we are going to raise your emotional governor so that you begin to reach and maintain higher levels of happiness.

BECOMING HAPPY THIS YEAR!

In Part One of this book, you will discover that what most people consider to be a major contributing factor in creating happiness holds little importance. And you will gain an insight into your new life as a happier person.

Parts Two and Three of this book are framed around a profound quotation that has been attributed to many different people, including the Taoist Lao-tzu. Meryl Streep recently popularized it in her portrayal of Margaret Thatcher in the film *The Iron Lady.* Unfortunately, the actual author may be lost to obscurity. Regardless of who first articulated these words in this way, it is an ideal framework for developing and maintaining higher levels of happiness.

Watch your thoughts, for they become words.
Watch your words, for they become actions.
Watch your actions, for they become habits.
Watch your habits, for they become character.
Watch your character, for it becomes your destiny.

We, alone, control our thoughts, our words, and our actions. As a result, our habits, character, and destiny are never set in stone. You can become happier. Your current level of happiness is simply that—your *current* level of happiness.

Consider the twin meanings of our word "current." It means both the way things are now, as in "the current situation," and it also means a flow, as in "a river current." Waiting downstream is your future life, and you can adjust how happy that life will be by choosing carefully the thoughts, words, and actions that you place into the current.

The English word "resolution" comes from the Latin *resolvere,* which actually means to untie, unfasten, loosen, or unbind. You may feel tied to your previous level of happiness and bound by your failures to follow through on previous resolutions. If so, it's time to unfasten your mind from the past, loosen your uncertainty, and unbind yourself from the way things have been.

It's nice to wish other people a "Happy New Year." However, it is far better to claim the coming New Year as the beginning of a higher and enduring level of happiness for yourself. Decide now that you will be happy *this* year!

Now, let's get happy.

PART ONE

Clarifying Happiness

My happiness is not the means to any end. It is the end. It is its own goal. It is its own purpose.
—Ayn Rand, *Anthem*

CHAPTER ONE

Can't Buy Me Happiness

Trying to be happy by accumulating possessions is like trying to satisfy hunger by taping sandwiches all over your body.
—George Carlin

During a recent visit to China, I enjoyed lunch as the guest of a wealthy Chinese entrepreneur. This man is in his early 40s and is already a billionaire, and his business continues to experience explosive growth.

After some genial conversation interpreted through our translator, this man, who lives what many would imagine to be an idyllic life, leaned over to me and whispered in broken English, "I'm not happy." His eyes were misty with tears of sad discontent, and he seemed to be subtly pleading for me to help him.

Of all the people I met on that trip, my interaction with this man impacted me the most. Why are this prosperous man and so many others like him, who seem to have every reason to be happy, struggling to enjoy their lives?

THE MONEY = HAPPINESS MYTH

A study published in the June 30, 2006, issue of *Science* found this: "The belief that high income is associated with good mood is widespread but mostly illusory. People with above-average income are relatively satisfied with their lives but are barely happier than others in moment-to-moment experience, tend to be more tense, and do not spend more time in particularly enjoyable activities."

It's been said a thousand ways, in every culture, and throughout history that money does not buy happiness. A Chinese proverb puts it this way:

> *With money you can buy a house, but not a home.*
> *With money you can buy a clock, but not time.*
> *With money you can buy a bed, but not sleep.*
> *With money you can buy a book, but not knowledge.*
> *With money you can buy a doctor, but not good health,*
> *With money you can buy a position, but not respect.*
> *With money you can buy blood, but not life,*
> *With money you can buy sex, but not love.*

And with money you can buy a great many things, but you cannot buy happiness.

Studies have found that a person who is abjectly poor can experience an increase in feeling happy when a higher level of income is reached—but only up to a point. Once he or she reaches a comfortable level of subsistence, more money has only a marginal bearing on happiness. In fact, greater wealth may have the opposite effect.

COULD MORE MONEY = LESS HAPPINESS?

According to the *World Happiness Report*, which was commissioned for a United Nations Conference on Happiness under the auspices of the UN General Assembly, "While higher income may raise happiness to some extent, the *quest* for higher income may actually reduce one's happiness."

That last part is especially significant.

People often misquote a verse from the Christian Bible. They will quip, "Money is the root of all evil." The actual quote from 1 Timothy 6:10 is, "The love of money is the root of all evil." *Loving* and pursuing money as an end unto itself rather than receiving money as the effect of living your life's purpose can actually make you *less* happy!

Nearly a half century ago, behavioral researchers conducted a study with a group of monkeys. The monkeys lived together in harmony and seemed quite content until one day the experimenters put a single toy into the cage. As one monkey began to play with the toy, the other monkeys first acted curious and then resentful. Ultimately, fighting broke out. A constant jockeying back and forth for possession of the toy ensued, resulting in a complete breakdown of their community.

The monkey who had the toy became stressed and anxious, perpetually on guard that another monkey would try and take it away. The monkeys who did not have the toy envied the one who did and spent their time either in sullen resignation or looking for an opportunity to steal it away. Prior to introduction of the toy, the monkeys spent hours grooming one another and playing happily. After the introduction of the toy, they became hostile and distrustful of one another.

The toy was not the cause of the monkey's discontent. It was their desire for the toy and their resentment that another monkey had what they did not. Comparing ourselves to others always leaves us discontented, regardless of how much we have.

GROSS NATIONAL HAPPINESS

In 1972, the fourth king of Bhutan coined a phrase that is rapidly becoming common around the world: "gross national happiness." The king stated that the true measurement of a country's greatness is more to be found in its gross national happiness (GNH) than in its gross national product (GNP).

In China, an exploding economy has led to the country now having more than one million millionaires. In fact, next to the United States and Japan, China has more millionaires than any other country. And, second only to the United States, China is home to the most billionaires in the world. A recent study found that there are 412 billionaires in China, which is more billionaires than in the next six countries combined, and yet China ranks a dismal 82nd in GNH.

The upsurge of wealth in China is not resulting in an increase in overall happiness. This supports the findings published in a 1974 paper titled "Does Economic Growth Improve the Human Lot? Some Empirical Evidence," by economist

Richard Easterlin of the University of Southern California. Easterlin found that as countries become richer, reported happiness does not increase. This has come to be known as the Easterlin Paradox.

"MONEY" AS A VERB

Perhaps the Chinese language perpetuates the confusion between more money and greater happiness. The Mandarin symbol *qián*, which denotes "money," is pronounced the same as the symbol that means "forward," "ahead," or "future." It is not surprising, therefore, that a Chinese person would believe that more and more money will yield greater and greater levels of happiness.

When a Chinese man or woman expresses anticipation for something—perhaps a new job or a happy marriage—it sounds like, "I 'money' to have a new job," or, "I 'money' a happy marriage." Because of the idiosyncrasies of the language, money and the positive feelings of attainment have become hopelessly intertwined.

Here in the United States the word "money" was similarly used for a time as a statement of appreciation. When people saw something they liked very much or experienced something that was particularly enjoyable, it was popular to say, "Man, that's money!"

THE BURDEN OF WEALTH

Beyond what we have been told by philosophers and spiritual leaders for millennia, we now know scientifically that more money does not mean more happiness. However, there is still a pervasive myth that higher levels of prosperity yield higher levels of happiness, and it is important to dispel this myth before we proceed.

Chances are that you, like most people, hold some remnant of this belief as well. Even though you know intellectually that more money won't make you happy, beneath the surface of your mind the idea persists that if you just had more money you'd be happier.

Actually, for some people, it's the other way around.

One study found that 1 in 10 people who accrue vast amounts of money become *less* happy as a result. A woman I know who amassed significant wealth over a short period of time told me, "Having a lot of money didn't eliminate all of my problems—it only eliminated *one* of my problems: a lack of money. And, honestly, sometimes having all that money can be a real pain in the neck!"

The burgeoning field of behavioral economics might help us understand why some people who become wealthy may become less happy as a result.

One of the findings of behavioral economics is that human beings tend to experience loss more deeply than they do gain. For example, suppose that you have a meter in your mind that measures contentment. Imagine that the needle on the meter is pointing straight up at zero—neutral. If you found $20 on the ground, your contentment meter might swing to the right and measure, say, a positive 10.

However, if you were to *lose* $20, your contentment meter might swing to the left from a neutral zero to a negative 20, or even more!

A *gain* of $20 moves your contentment a positive 10 points whereas a *loss* of $20 moves your contentment needle a negative 20 points. The amount of money is the same, but whether you are losing or gaining the cash significantly varies your emotional response.

Legendary sportscaster Vin Scully succinctly described this aspect of behavioral economics. With respect to sports, he said, "Losing feels worse than winning feels good."

When people earn or inherit large amounts of money, they often begin to fear the pain of losing what they now possess.

Think of it this way. A person standing on the bottom rung of a very tall ladder has only a minimal fear of falling to the ground, because the distance is quite short. Chances are very slight that he or she will experience much pain from falling from such a distance.

A person lacking wealth, therefore, is not as consumed with losing his or her meager possessions. As the old saying goes, "When you've got nothing, you've got nothing to lose." However, a person who has climbed the very same ladder to a rung 50 feet above the ground would be far more concerned about falling.

When you understand that people experience loss more intensely than they do gain, and that a person with a lot of money has more to lose, it becomes understandable why more money may actually make some people feel less happy.

OTHER FACTORS

There are other factors that can contribute to a person who becomes wealthy reporting lower levels of subjective well-being.

For some, there can be a perceived loss of authentic relationships with other people that may lead to a feeling of disconnection and abandonment. I once heard megastar Eddie Murphy lament that when he had become rich and famous, he had hired all of his friends and family to work for him. He moved from being their friend and relative to being their employer, which dramatically altered their relationship. He grieved the fact that neither his family nor his friends would provide him honest feedback, as they had when he was a just a struggling young comedian.

A significant increase in prosperity can also raise the fear that others might try to take our wealth from us. Think of the stress endured by the monkeys that possessed the toy the others wanted. They were always on guard to protect it lest another monkey try to steal it away.

There is yet another reason why having lots of money might actually lower a person's happiness level. Significant increases in wealth or income can call forth a feeling of unworthiness. A person may not feel deserving of such a high level of affluence, which can create a burning discomfort.

This internal angst may cause him or her to act out in negative ways toward others. Friends, family, and coworkers may mistakenly interpret this behavior as the person's newfound wealth spawning an overly inflated sense of importance. In reality, the opposite is true. It has brought to the surface a latent feeling of inadequacy.

In his book *The Big Leap*, Gay Hendricks explains that each of us has what he calls an "Upper Limit switch." When we experience a significant increase in income or something else great happens in our lives, the switch gets tripped, causing us to feel anxious, and so we often create problems to reduce the tension of life being better than we feel we deserve.

SPIRITUALITY—A BRIDGE BETWEEN MONEY AND HAPPINESS

Does this all mean we can't have money and be happy? Are we doomed to be like the legendary Greek king Midas, who was given the power to turn anything he touched into gold but starved to death because whenever he touched food it became solid metal?

I don't believe so. In fact, there is a recipe for having both wealth and happiness.

According to the *World Happiness Report*, "The beneficial development of human society takes place when material and spiritual development occurs side by side to complement and reinforce each other."

Not surprisingly, explosive levels of prosperity in China are creating a vacuum for spirituality. An article in the March 9, 2006, *Christian Science Monitor*, states, "As China becomes more wealthy and worldly, it's also experiencing a growing interest in spirituality."

Let's be careful not to confuse spirituality with religion. Religion and spirituality are not always synonymous.

Religion can often be exclusive, whereas spirituality is inclusive. Many studies have shown that a person who nurtures a spiritual connection—that is, a realization of the oneness of all things and the interconnectedness of all people—tends to be happier, regardless of his or her income level.

If my command of the Chinese language were better, I would have asked my wealthy but unfulfilled lunch host how much meaning and internal satisfaction he derived from his business. I would have explored how deeply he felt connected to other people as a result of his endeavors.

During our conversation, this man had expressed with understandable pride how his company had grown, but I did not hear him share the positive impact his organization was having on the lives of his customers and employees. If we could have spoken candidly and at length, I would have encouraged him to seek out a deeper purpose for himself and his company—a purpose that is about making a difference.

Rather than placing his focus so intensely on growth and increased profits, I would have asked this man to take a step back and see how his company and the products and services it provides can improve the lives of his customers, and to immediately begin to make this as an equal priority with profitability.

In addition, I would have suggested that this Chinese billionaire look deeply into how his organization could become a catalyst for improving the lives of its employees.

Another Chinese national now residing in America has built the fastest-growing chain of Chinese restaurants in the United States by making his employees' lives his primary focus.

Andrew Cherng, the founder of Panda Express, set an intention to not only build a national chain of high-quality Chinese restaurants but also to make it an explicit goal to improve the lives of his employees in the process, as expressed in the Panda Express mission statement:

Deliver exceptional Asian dining experiences by building an organization where people are inspired to better their lives.

How has this worked out for Cherng? In just over 30 years trying to gain market share in the highly competitive US fast-food market, Panda Express has grown from a single store in Pasadena, California, to more than 1,400 stores in 43 states with revenues nearly triple those of its next two competitors combined. According to *USA Today*, Panda Express opens more than three new restaurants every week!

A couple of years back, I met Cherng at one of his restaurants and we talked briefly. Here was a man who is quite wealthy and yet seems to bubble over with happiness, because his focus is as much or more on his mission to improve the lives of his employees as on his company's growth and profits. In addition to external wealth, Cherng enjoys internal prosperity.

MAKE YOUR PURPOSE YOUR TARGET

There is an ancient story said to have been about the life of the young Indian prince Siddhārtha Gautama. The legend says that the young prince was a master at archery, and whenever a contest was held, Prince Siddhartha would always win first prize. The medals the young prince received for winning the many competitions covered one of the palace walls.

After losing yet again to the prince, a frustrated competitor threw his bow to the ground and demanded to know the secret to the prince's uncanny ability to win every time.

The prince proffered a smile of compassion and answered softly, "I aim for the target."

"I also aim for the target!" spat the man indignantly.

"No," said the prince, "you aim for the medals and, as a result, you miss the target. I aim for the target and, as a result, I win the medals."

Prince Siddhartha would later be known by a far loftier title: the Buddha.

Focus on your sacred purpose and you will enjoy, and quite probably increase, the rewards you receive. Focus on the rewards alone and they will never be enough.

The human desire to obtain more is a sieve that can never be filled with all the water from the world's oceans. As we acquire more, we always want more. The Hindu sacred text *Śrīmad Bhāgavatam* puts it this way: "Never can desire be quenched by repeated enjoyment of desires; like butter poured on a fire with a view to quenching it, desire only gets inflamed thereby."

CHINESE SUPERHEROES

I began this chapter with a story about a wealthy man I met in China. There is another aspect of becoming wealthy that can play against a person living in that country. Chinese culture is based on Confucian teachings that emphasize the needs of society over the needs of the individual.

In much of Asia, individualism is downplayed. This is evidenced by the Japanese saying "The nail that stands out gets hammered down."

During one of my visits to China, an interpreter asked me lots of questions about American superheroes. Having been raised on Captain America comic books, the *Batman* television show, and movies about Superman, Spider-Man, and others, I was enthusiastic to talk about our superheroes.

After a lengthy conversation, I said, "Tell me about Chinese superheroes."

"There aren't any," she responded.

"Come on!" I said. "There must be *some* Chinese superheroes."

"No," she replied. "In America, the individual is celebrated and so a superhero that surpasses everyone else is an inspiring part of your culture. In China, a person who excels beyond others is often scorned."

In his book *China Shakes the World*, author James Kynge tells of visiting China in the 1960s. At that time, he noticed that everyone wore black and white because no one wanted to stand out. Later that decade, he noticed a subtle shift as some people began to wear navy blue rather than black. Today, he notes, people are beginning to dress in colors that represent their tastes and individuality, and this is leading to some nagging feelings of discomfort and even guilt.

When people—be they Chinese, American, or any nationality—begin to enjoy higher levels of prosperity, their lifestyles set them apart from others within their circle of friends and family. And, because a sense of interconnectedness with others has been shown to fortify feelings of happiness, this can pose a threat to one's increased sense of well-being.

If you wish to become happy, understand that the first step is to *really know* that, regardless of your level of prosperity, you will always want more money—but that the additional money will not provide a corresponding increase in your happiness. Billionaire record executive and film producer David Geffen put it well: "Anybody who thinks money will make you happy hasn't got money."

A NOTE OF CAUTION

Even as you begin to grasp that happiness and money are not the same, recognize that there are forces at work that will continue to try to get you to equate the two.

Consider advertising campaigns. For example, a person in a commercial who buys a new car is always shown smiling happily. The underlying message of the advertisement: a new car equals happiness, and the more expensive the car, the greater the happiness. The promise of increased happiness is a powerful manipulator, so be on your guard.

A February 6, 2006, article published in the magazine *Fast Company* quotes James Roberts, a Baylor University marketing professor: "The research is overwhelmingly clear. The more materialistic you are the less happy you are. We get Happiness through the love of others and sense of community. But we've been told by Madison Avenue that Happiness can come through the mall."

American journalist George Lorimer wrote, "It's a good thing to have money and the things that money can buy, but it's good, too, to check up once in a while and make sure you haven't lost the things that money can't buy."

Now that we've cleared up the "more money means greater happiness" myth, let's increase the most valuable thing money *can't* buy—your happiness!

RECAPPING "CAN'T BUY ME HAPPINESS"

- Whether or not you are aware of it, you probably have some latent belief in the myth that more money will lead to greater happiness.
- Without a solid foundation in happiness, increased prosperity can actually lessen your overall happiness.

- Living your purpose leads to happiness; profit alone does not.

- People experience loss more intensely than they experience gain.

- The economy runs on materialism. Materialism runs on the myth that more money and more possessions equal more happiness.

CHAPTER TWO

You > Happy

The secret of achievement is to hold a picture of a successful outcome in the mind.
—Henry David Thoreau

A while back, a man came to me for counseling. He was unhappy in his career and wanted to make a change. He had been a very successful photographer specializing in family portraits and weddings, but he no longer found any fulfillment in his work.

"What would you do if all jobs paid the same?" I asked. "In other words, what would you *like* to do?"

Considering what he might enjoy doing for a living rather than what he *had* done or what others felt he *should* do took awhile.

At length he responded, "I still love photography. I guess I'd like to travel and shoot pictures of classic cars and motorcycles, creating custom calendars and other products for collectors."

"Then get started," I said.

"Oh, I just can't see myself doing that," he said.

"That's the problem," I said. "If you can't see yourself doing it, you don't have a compelling vision pulling you toward your dream. If you don't see your destination, you're bound to get lost or give up."

Can you see yourself as a happy person? Can you see what your life will be like when you are living the happy life you aspire to live? German philosopher Immanuel Kant stated that, "Happiness is not an ideal of reason but of imagination." You are reading this book because you want to become a happier person, but chances are you have never used the power of your imagination to get a clear image of what a happier version of you would be like.

In this chapter, you are going to discern your current level of happiness and create a vision of your new happy life so that everything else in this book becomes a brick creating a solid foundation for that vision.

We're going to engage in two exercises. The first will take a couple of minutes each day. The second exercise will require a one-time commitment of between 10 and 20 minutes.

Don't skip over these exercises! They are powerful first steps toward becoming a happier person.

CALCULATING HAPPINESS

The brilliant Russian author Fyodor Dostoyevsky observed, "Man only likes to count his troubles; he doesn't calculate his happiness."

Most people count their troubles and, as a result, they are not nearly as happy as they might be. To get happier, begin to calculate your happiness.

Just How Happy Are You?

On a scale from 1 to 10, how happy would you say you are right now? Don't overthink this; simply guesstimate how happy you feel right now. And remember, it's called "subjective well-being," because *you* alone can say how happy you are.

Next, during the upcoming week, check in with yourself a few times each day and write down your level of happiness each time. Optimally, you should do this three times per day at the same time each day.

To help you remember, consider doing this at "Dr Pepper times." You may have no idea what the term "Dr Pepper times" means, but when I was a boy, the popular soft drink Dr Pepper had the numbers 10, 2, and 4 printed in big red letters on its label.

The origin of these numbers dates back to the 1930s when J. B. O'Hara, an employee of the company, discovered that many people reported an energy lull at 10:30 a.m., 2:30 p.m., and 4:30 p.m.. Because Dr Pepper contained sugar and caffeine, it provided a jolt of energy. O'Hara suggested that the company market to consumers that drinking Dr Pepper at 10 a.m., 2 p.m., and 4 p.m. would help them avoid a dip in energy. Dr Pepper was marketed as one of the first energy drinks.

Mark your calendar or set a computer or smartphone reminder at Dr Pepper times—10 a.m., 2 p.m., and 4 p.m., or whatever times you want. Ask yourself how happy you feel on a scale from 1 (very unhappy) to 10 (ecstatically happy) three times each day and write down your answers.

Your Average Happiness Level

At the end of each week, average your answers to get an idea of your happiness level for that week. For example, if you noted your happiness level a total of 21 times (that's three times a day for seven days), add your ratings together and divide by 21 to get your average happiness level.

Next, set a happiness goal for the following week and repeat the exercise.

You may be wondering, "Does he want me to do this every week?"

The answer is *yes.*

Doing this on an ongoing basis will take you *less than five minutes per week* and it can dramatically increase your level of happiness.

Become 19% Happier

One study on subjective well-being found that just being mindful of your level of happiness could cause it to increase. Setting a goal for your happiness level and then checking to see how you're doing is like setting a goal weight and then stepping on the bathroom scale to see where you are relative to your goal.

I tested this concept with 18 people in a simple, nonscientific study. I emailed a dozen or so friends and family members asking if they wanted to participate in a happiness experiment. Twelve of them responded saying that they would be involved and another half dozen of their friends opted to join in as well.

At the beginning of each week I emailed each of my 18 subjects and asked them to set a goal as to how happy they would like to average during the upcoming week on a scale from 1 (very unhappy) to 10 (ecstatically happy). I then sent each of them a text three times each day asking them to rate their current level of happiness.

At the end of the week, I sent each person an email saying, for example, "Your happiness goal for this week was a 9 and you averaged an 8.5." I then asked each person to set a happiness goal for the following week and we repeated the process.

Here's how it turned out: at the end of three weeks, 100% of participants reported being, on average, nearly 19% happier than when we began!

Now I know that for many reasons this would not be considered a formal scientific experiment. I also know that asking people a question about something actually causes them to begin to look for what is being inquired about and, as a result, it makes them more aware of it. That is to say, encouraging someone to set a happiness goal and then repeatedly asking how happy he or she is tends to make the person seem happier because the focus is on happiness—and that's the point!

Happiness and unhappiness are not only mental states, they are also mental evaluations. To paraphrase Dostoyevsky, as you begin to calculate your happiness level rather than counting your troubles, you will begin to feel happier.

It all comes down to where you are focusing your thoughts.

Consider this: If I were to text you three times each day and ask you to report back how many red objects are within your current field of vision, you would become much more aware of the color red, not only when you received the texts but throughout the day as well. Because you are repeatedly being asked about the color red, it would be in the forefront of your mind.

Best-selling author and thought leader Deepak Chopra explains why this happens: "Simply by becoming more aware, you become a powerful agent of change. There is no need to force anything, only to expand your awareness."

Setting a happiness goal and then checking in with yourself to see how happy you are keeps your awareness on happiness, and you begin to see more happiness-inducing experiences.

So, every single person who participated in my little experiment set a weekly happiness goal and we kept track of his or her happiness level three times a day. As a result, they all became, on average, almost 20% happier, right? But what if they were just reporting increasingly higher levels of happiness because they thought doing so would, well, make *me* happy? Many of these people knew me and were aware that I was testing a hypothesis on happiness. Perhaps this tainted their responses. For this reason, I decided to put some distance between the participants and myself by sending out a follow-up survey so that each person could anonymously share whether he or she felt that the exercise had increased his or her level of happiness. I told everyone that I would have no way of knowing how each person responded to the survey.

Their responses to the survey revealed that nearly 80% felt that this practice had increased their level of happiness.

Two Types of Happiness

An article from the April 6, 2012, edition of the *Economist* reports, "Researchers break down people's feelings into 'affective happiness' (everyday ups and downs) and 'evaluative happiness' (a person's overall assessment of his or her life)." You are going to experience ups and downs in your life. But taking time to evaluate your level of happiness places your focus on happiness and will cause it to increase.

What would you do for a boost of nearly 20% in your happiness level? Investing just five minutes a week to set a happiness goal and monitor your progress can make it happen.

WHAT DO *YOU* MEAN BY "BEING HAPPY?"

To become happier, you need to get an image in your mind of how your life will be when you consistently average a higher happiness set point.

Again, to equate happiness to fitness, if you wanted to lose weight and get in shape, you would first determine what you mean by "getting in shape." To do this, you would imagine a fit version of yourself and consider, "How much would this healthier version of me weigh?" "What would I look like?" And, possibly, "How would I feel?" You might even get a clear mental image of your fit and trim self at the store trying on new clothes or perhaps walking proudly along the beach in a swimsuit. You would use the power of your imagination to clarify and inspire yourself to get in shape.

A Personal Story

As a teenager, I was very obese. My senior year in high school I lost more than one hundred pounds. Unfortunately, as the years passed, I slowly gained back nearly half the weight I had lost. I began to feel uncomfortable, my clothes were tight, and whenever I leaned over to tie my shoes, I groaned from the exertion.

I resolved to lose some weight and get in shape, and used my imagination to reach my goal.

First, I stepped on my bathroom scale and weighed myself; I had put this off because I really didn't want to acknowledge how out of shape I had become. Once I faced the truth of my situation, I decided exactly how much I intended to weigh.

To ignite my imagination, I stepped back on the scale but this time I had a camera with me. I aimed the camera down and took a photo of my feet on either side of the digital readout that displayed my current weight. I then loaded the picture onto my computer and used an image-editing software program to place my goal weight on the image of the digital readout. I printed the picture out and posted it next to my computer so that I would see it every day while I worked.

Because I knew clearly what I meant by "lose weight" and had imagined a positive result, I ultimately achieved my goal.

Arnold's Secret to Success

When it comes to being in shape, few people have had the single-minded focus of Arnold Schwarzenegger. The bodybuilder/actor/politician won 24 bodybuilding titles, including six Mr. Olympia crowns. Throughout his bodybuilding career, Schwarzenegger had a ritual of taking monthly photos of himself. He would then take a red pen and mark on the pictures the parts of his body that he felt needed improvement. Based on his intention, Arnold would change his nutrition and exercise regimens to sculpt his idea of the perfect body.

For Arnold, being "in shape" was something he had quantified and held firmly in his mind before he ever entered the gym. His imagination guided his every action.

"I want to lose weight" or "I want to get in shape" are far too vague to hold your attention and keep you motivated. Similarly, to state "I want to be happy" is impotent and open to miles of interpretation.

See Your Future, Be Your Future

This exercise, whose name I coined from a Chevy Chase line in *Caddyshack*, helps you paint a clear mental image of what you will be like as a happier person, which will, in turn, guide and inspire your progress.

It is very important to invest 10 to 20 minutes *now* answering these questions. Without a clear idea of what your life will be like as a happier person, you will find that you are aiming at a target while blindfolded.

First, close your eyes and picture yourself six months in the future. Imagine that your new happiness set point is two or three points higher than it is now. Now, from this imagined perspective, answer these questions:

- *As a happier person, specifically, how is your life different?*
- *How have your relationships improved?*
- *When challenging situations arise, how do you maintain this higher level of happiness?*
- *How has your homelife improved?*
- *How have things at work improved?*
- *As a happier person, how do you tend to act toward others?*
- *How do other people treat you?*
- *Imagine you find a camera with dozens of candid photos taken of the new happier you. How do you look? What is your expression? When you look into your own eyes, what do you see?*
- *How do you feel?*
- *What is the greatest improvement you have seen in your life as a result of becoming happier?*

Now that you have answered these questions, bookmark this page and invest 60 seconds reading your answers every morning. This will not only keep you on track to becoming a happier person, it will keep you inspired along your journey.

The Buddy System

To get the most out of these two exercises, find a "Happiness Buddy"—a friend or family member who not only supports you in your quest to become happier but who also would like to measurably and sustainably increase his or her own level of happiness.

Share your answers to the questions in the second exercise with your Happiness Buddy; you can then remind each other what your motivations are for becoming happier and give each other support.

On Sunday afternoons, share your happiness goal for the coming week with your Happiness Buddy. Then, call, text, email, or otherwise connect three times each day to share your current happiness level with each other. Becoming happier means developing a new habit of happiness, and studies have found that having someone to walk with you on your path to creating a new habit greatly increases your likelihood of success.

In *The Power of Habit,* author and *New York Times* business writer Charles Duhigg explains that having a support structure when making a significant life change is the reason both Weight Watchers and Alcoholics Anonymous have been so successful. A partner to share your happiness journey means someone to encourage you and to hold you accountable. Whether you are trying to lose weight, overcome an addiction to alcohol, or fulfill your resolution to become a happier person, there is no substitute for having someone to share your voyage.

When I became committed to losing weight and getting in shape, I reached out to a friend who lives two thousand miles away. Every day, he and I would send each other a brief email detailing what we had eaten that day, as well as a synopsis of that day's exercise regimen.

What a difference this made! In short order, we both got in great shape.

Make it your resolution to be happy first and you will find that the other things you desire come to you more easily as a natural result of your increased sense of well-being. Furthermore, and much more important, you will more fully enjoy the other improvements you make in your life, which will increase the likelihood that they will endure.

RECAPPING "YOU ▸ HAPPY"

- At the beginning of each week, set a happiness goal level.

- Check in with yourself a few times each day to see how happy you are. Keep a record of your happiness level and compare your average to your weekly goal.

- Get a clear mental picture of what your life will be like when you are significantly happier. Hold this image in your mind as often as possible.

- Find a Happiness Buddy who wants both of you to become happier. Check in with him or her daily.

PART TWO

Mastering the Causes of Happiness

A tree that can fill the span of a man's arms grows from a downy tip; a terrace nine stories high rises from hodfuls of earth; a journey of a thousand miles starts from beneath one's feet.
—Lao-tzu

CHAPTER THREE

Thoughts of Happiness

Very little is needed to make a happy life; it is all within yourself, in your way of thinking.
—Marcus Aurelius

Your brain is relatively small, weighing only about three pounds. However, your brain's thoughts direct the actions of your entire body and steer the course of your life. The relationship between your brain and your body is comparable to the relationship between a 180-pound pilot flying a 220,000-pound jet. For all of its mass and power, the jet will only go as the pilot directs it.

For a safe and smooth flight, a competent pilot is crucial. For a happy life, happy thoughts are the first step.

There is no happiness outside of happy mind-set. To reach a higher sustainable level of happiness, you must begin to change your thoughts so that they are in line with those of a happy person.

Happiness is relative and subjective, and it is because of this that we can change our thoughts and, thereby, bend our perception to raise our happiness set point.

HONK IF YOU'RE HAPPY

I once lived in South Carolina and made my living selling insurance door-to-door. I would often drive up and down Highway 544 between Conway and Surfside Beach, calling on customers.

One day I spotted a sign crudely scribbled on cardboard, stuck into the ground next to this busy highway; it read "Honk if you're happy." I discovered that when I drove by this sign and honked my horn, my level of happiness increased.

Did the sign somehow magically imbue me with increased happiness? No. My happiness level did an uptick because when I saw it, I began to think about being happy.

The shift occurred in my mind. Happiness is not only a mental state, it is a mental evaluation. The very first line of the Buddhist Dhammapada explains the relationship between the use of our minds and the mind's perception: "Mind precedes all mental states." In other words, thinking precedes all thoughts. And, happy thinking yields happy thoughts.

THE FLOW OF THOUGHT ENERGY

Thought energy flows in two directions. It projects out and it receives back. Your mind sends out what you expect to experience and then reports back what actually occurs.

The path to higher levels of sustainable happiness lies in taking intentional control of our thoughts and placing a far greater emphasis on what goes out than what comes in—that is, sending out thoughts that represent the happy life you would like to live rather than settling for what you currently experience.

In time, reality will catch up with your happier thoughts— you will begin to live in the positive world you have been imagining. Your thoughts will then feed off of this positive input and mix with your positive output. Optimal living becomes habitual and the process becomes self-perpetuating.

If you go back to the idea that you have a predominant average of your overall happiness, you can use controlled thought process to increase the height of the highest range and also shorten the duration of the lowest. As I'll demonstrate, this will lead to a cascading effect of happiness throughout your life.

THE BEST VITAMIN TO BE A HAPPY PERSON IS B1

The prolific Roman philosopher Publilius Syrus wrote, "No man is happy who does not think himself so." As mentioned previously, happiness and unhappiness are not just mental states; they are mental evaluations.

In talking to happy people, I have found that, without exception, they define themselves as being happy.

Happiness is a conscious choice. It is a way of describing yourself, and when you begin to describe yourself as happy, you will begin to find supporting evidence for your being happy.

"I'm Happy To..."

During my most recent speaking trip to China, I stayed in a hotel that was in the process of renovating its health club. I went down to the front desk and inquired if there might be somewhere else I could go to get in a workout. The concierge informed me that the hotel had an arrangement with a nearby health club and that a member of the hotel's fitness staff would escort me to the facility.

The first thing I noticed about the young man who went with me to the health club was his broad and beaming smile. I had met many happy people in China, but this guy gushed happiness.

Because of the increasing number of business connections being made between East and West, many Chinese are adopting American- or European-sounding first names for dealing with people from English-speaking countries. Sometimes, either to be unique or out of a lack of understanding of given names common in the West, some Chinese take on some rather unusual names.

The young man who worked for the hotel's fitness staff had chosen a first name that is a common word in the West but very atypical as a name. His last name is "Tu" and the first he selected is "Happy." Therefore, his name is "Happy Tu."

In the West, when we ask someone if he or she is willing do something, the individual may respond, "I'm happy to," showing enthusiastic willingness. Without knowing it, Happy Tu had put together a name of such joyful service that whenever people from English-speaking countries met him, they treated him as if he was indeed happy, gracious, and friendly. As a result, he reflected these characteristics back.

"Hi, My Name Is Happy"

Are you a happy person? Would you describe yourself as a happy person? If you adopted the first name "Happy," would it be a fit for you?

How does it feel right now to say "I am a happy person"? Give it a try. Say it aloud: "I am happy." If it feels natural and like a match for you, then you are well on your way, because you have a solid foundation for happiness. If you're like most people, however, you'll feel some resistance, and it's this resistance we are going to eradicate.

Confucius said, "We take greater pains to persuade others we are happy than in trying to think so ourselves." The more you can convince yourself that you are happy, the happier you become.

Simply running the words "I am happy," "I am happy," "I am happy" over and over through your mind causes you to begin to feel happy. One reason this works is that by repeatedly affirming that you are happy, your mind will eventually think, "So, I'm happy, huh? Well, *why* am I happy?" This question will then cause you to seek out things that are going well in your life rather than the handful of challenges that tend to dominate your thinking, and you will feel happier.

Be careful not to say "I want to be happy." When you say "I want to be happy," you are affirming that you are *not* happy. Think about it this way: If you already have something, you don't yearn for it. If, however, you want something, it means you don't have it. Stating that you want happiness means you are admitting that you don't have happiness and, because happiness is a mental evaluation, you drive it further away from you.

Measure How High You Are, Not How High You Aren't

Remember, happiness levels exist along a continuum from 1 to 10. Although we all dip down to a level 1 (very unhappy) from time to time, we rarely stay there for long. As you evaluate your happiness level, you can choose to feel resentment for how far you are below a 10. Or, you can choose to be grateful for how far you are above a 1. This acknowledgment of how happy you are—rather than condemnation of how happy you are not—will raise your awareness and feeling of happiness.

"Wait a minute!" you may be thinking. "I thought you were going to teach me how to be happy. It sounds like you're just trying to get me to delude myself into believing that I already *am* happy."

To which I respond, "Yep—they are one and the same."

One of the definitions of "delusion" is "a belief that has been surrendered to and accepted by the whole mind as a truth." Both happiness and unhappiness are, in many ways, delusions—something we have surrendered to and accepted in our minds as true.

Your evaluative level of happiness is, in many ways, a decision you make. It has little to do with your situation. Two people in identical situations can delude themselves into feeling happy or unhappy. The situation is the same; the only difference is their thinking.

In act 2, scene 2 of Shakespeare's *Hamlet*, Hamlet says to Rosencrantz and Guildenstern, "For there is nothing either good or bad, but thinking makes it so." You are what you describe yourself to be. If you think you are happy, you are.

If you say "I am happy," you will begin to feel and act happy, and the world will reflect this back to you, which will increase your feeling of happiness. If, however, you say "I *want* to be happy," you are designating yourself as wanting in the area of happiness and happiness will elude you.

Simmer Happiness While You Sleep

Affirm as often as you can, "I am happy." Say it while you drive, clean your house, or take a shower. It is especially important for you to say it over and over as you are drifting off to sleep.

Your subconscious never sleeps. Unfortunately, many of us lie in bed at night replaying the unpleasant events of the day in our minds or, worse, imagining distressing and even possibly dire scenarios that might happen the following day.

We do this night after night and then wonder why we are not happier.

This is like placing spoiled ingredients into a Crock-Pot to simmer for eight hours and then wondering why the resulting meal is distasteful.

In his book *Wishes Fulfilled*, Wayne Dyer quotes the great twentieth-century metaphysician Neville Goddard, "Whatever you have in consciousness as you go to sleep is the measure of your expression in the waking two-thirds of your life on earth." If you affirm that you are happy as you enter into the one-third of your life where your body sleeps but where your mind continues to simmer, you will discover that you will experience greater happiness.

Dyer writes, "In presleep moments, you can program your subconscious to automatically present you with fulfilled wishes." If your wish is to be happier, program your subconscious to believe that you are already happy and then remind yourself that this is so throughout the day with the affirmations "I am happy!" and "I am a happy person!"

Many people find that they awaken in the morning at their lowest happiness level. This is because they go to sleep fretting over what is to come or replaying negative events that have transpired.

As you lie in bed at night, don't count sheep to fall asleep. Instead, count things for which you are grateful. Run things through your mind that bring you happiness and you will awaken at a higher happiness level the following morning. That happier mood will be easier to maintain throughout your day.

How Am I? I'm Happy!

When you meet someone and he or she asks, "How are you?" forego the typical and automatic response, "Fine." Instead, say "I'm happy!" Own your happiness! Notice how this increases your feeling of happiness and notice the big smile others will send your way when they hear you respond this way.

Master motivator Dale Carnegie wrote, "Remember, happiness doesn't depend upon who you are or what you have, it depends solely upon what you think." If you think you are happy, if you define yourself as being happy, you will be happy.

TAKING CHARGE OF YOUR MENTAL SPACE

Monkey mind, the ego, the separated self, whatever you call it—this is the critical inner voice that incites negative internal chatter in your head, questioning your abilities and your worth. This voice can be vicious, telling you that you don't deserve to be happy, that you are incapable of success, that you are unattractive, that you are inherently bad, and a variety of other hurtful and negative things.

You cannot maximize your level of happiness when this cruel and critical voice is running unchecked in your head.

Everyone has this voice, and it can be downright brutal. This voice is particularly accomplished at limiting your happiness because:

1. It knows all of your perceived inadequacies as well as your previous failures
2. It comes from within your own mind and sounds like you. As a result, you tend to believe it.

Your Rude Roommate

The negative voice that you hear is *not* you. It comes from negative things you have been told and/or believed about yourself, and its power has been compounded by its very existence.

Because happiness is a result of what you think, it is difficult, if not impossible, to feel happy with a constant negative voice track buzzing like angry bees in your mind. And, because it seems to be your own voice, it can be difficult to ignore.

Think of your mind as a home in which you live. You don't live alone. You share this space with a rude roommate known as your ego. It delivers judgmental and hurtful comments about you and others throughout the day.

I have a visual image I like to use when thinking of my ego. Johnny Knoxville played a character named Scrad in the movie *Men in Black II.* Scrad was a young man who went about his days enduring the incessant commentary of a second head that dangled back and forth over his shoulder on a long serpentine neck. Whatever Scrad was doing, the second head had something to say, typically something sarcastic and negative.

Knoxville played both the character Scrad and Scrad's second head. The two looked and sounded the same. The challenge with our ego is that it sounds like us.

Bart Simpson Thinks You're a Loser, Dude

To exorcise this demon, you must first separate it out as the distinct entity it truly is. When negative or limiting thoughts arise, begin to restate them in your mind in a voice that is clearly not your own and which you can more easily denounce.

Try any distinctive voice—the more irritating the better. Consider using Mickey Mouse or Goofy, Bart Simpson, Pee-wee Herman, Bobcat Goldthwait, Fran Drescher, Gilbert Gottfried (former voice of the Aflac duck), Jaleel White (as Steve Urkel from the TV show *Family Matters*), Megan Mullally (as Karen Walker from *Will & Grace*)—the voice doesn't matter. Just pick a voice that you can more readily dismiss than your own, and when you have a negative thought about yourself, play it over in your mind in the voice you have chosen. Better yet, *speak it aloud*, doing your best impression of the voice you have selected.

In their excellent book, *Conquer your Critical Inner Voice*, authors Robert Firestone, Lisa Firestone, Joyce Catlett, and Pat Love say that the key to winning out over the negative internal monster that haunts your psyche is to take it to task when it presents disapproving, pessimistic, hurtful, and limiting thoughts.

When the critical inner voice attacks, offer evidence to counter its assault. For example, if you are getting ready to go to a party and are feeling a little anxious, your ego might whisper something to the effect of this: "You're nervous about going to the party because you are socially awkward."

Identify this as the voice of the ego, imagine this comment being said in the voice and manner of, perhaps, Bart Simpson, and argue the point aloud.

Speak in your best Bart Simpson impression: "You're a total spaz at parties, dude!"

Respond calmly, clearly, and with authority in your own voice, "Everyone is uncomfortable when they first get together with other people—that's why most people tend to drink alcohol; so they can relax. I am not awkward, I'm just like everyone else, and if I just give it time, I will relax and settle into being at this party and I'll have fun."

This technique has immediate and almost magical results, and over time your inner critic, having been identified, separated out, and taken to task, will assault you less and less. When it has been caught, its attacks will diminish in occurrence and severity. Even though it will never fully go away, it will begin to diminish significantly.

Quip writer Cullen Hightower wrote, "Our ego is our silent partner. . .too often with a controlling interest." The ego's power comes from hiding in the shadows of our minds where it can appear to be larger and more important and, as a result, where it can impact our happiness. Forcing the ego into the light by giving it a distinct and grating voice allows us to sweep it aside and, in so doing, to raise our level of happiness.

TAMING YOUR THOUGHTS

Thus far, you've been encouraged to claim that you are a happy person and to actively dissociate from your ego mind. You may find that directing the course of your thoughts is more difficult than you would have imagined. However, it is possible to tame your mind so that it begins to move in the direction you choose, rather than running amuck.

Monty Roberts, the world-famous horse trainer, has helped tens of thousands of horse owners around the world convert untamed and seemingly untamable horses into gentle and well-trained equestrian partners. His method mirrors the innate socialization practices of horses in the wild.

First, Roberts puts the "green" horse into a large round pen and then attempts to approach the animal. If the horse acts in a threatening or disrespectful manner, such as turning its back in preparation for kicking, Roberts throws the heavy end of a weighted rope at the horse's rump, driving the horse away. A coil of rope thrown at the hindquarters of a 1,200-pound horse is not going to cause any harm, but it does shock the horse into flight.

Roberts continues to gather the rope up and then toss it at the horse's rump, forcing the horse to run in circles inside the pen. When the horse drops its head and begins to lick its lips—an act of submission and respect—Roberts extends the back of his hand, inviting the horse to come closer. If the horse balks or acts aggressively, the rope is again thrown and the process is repeated until the horse adopts a willing and compliant manner.

Right now, your mind may appear to be an untamed and, possibly, raging wild horse. It may seem nearly impossible to get your thoughts to go in the direction you want.

It is possible and, if you're willing to put forth a little effort, you can master your mind.

One Thing All Spiritual Masters Have in Common

Let's remember the quote from the *World Happiness Report* mentioned in Chapter 1 of this book: "The beneficial development of human society takes place when material and spiritual development occurs side by side to complement and reinforce each other."

If you study the great spiritual masters, you will realize that they all had one thing in common: meditation. Jesus of Nazareth regularly went off into the wilderness to sit quietly (meditate), and it is nearly impossible to find an image of the Buddha where he is not seated in silent meditation.

Today, even corporations are embracing the power of meditation. Google offers free meditation classes for each of its more than 35,000 employees and maintains meditation rooms at its facilities.

The following meditation practice will not only help you gain control over your thoughts, but it will also deepen your sense of spirituality—both of which will lead to increased and lasting feelings of happiness.

- Begin by finding a time when you will not be disturbed for at least 10 minutes—first thing in the morning is best. The longer you can meditate, the better, but starting with just 10 minutes will have a powerful impact on your happiness.

- Sit comfortably with your spine erect. Place your hands in your lap, palms facing up. Touch together the thumb and index finger of your right hand. Let your left hand remain open and relaxed.

- Take three long, slow, deep breaths. As you exhale the third time, gently close your eyes.

- Breathe consciously, deeply, and rhythmically inhaling and exhaling only through your nose. Focus your mind on the activity of breathing. Notice the sound your breath makes as it goes in and out. Notice the sensation of air moving across your upper lip. Feel your stomach move in and out as you breathe. Focus on only one thing: breathing.

- Keep track of how many consecutive breaths you take while *thinking only about the process of breathing.* If you are able to complete one entire breath only thinking about the act of breathing, move your right thumb to the middle finger of your right hand. If you complete a second breath thinking only about the action of breathing, move your thumb to the ring finger of your right hand, and then to your pinkie finger for yet another breath. This keeps track of your success and helps you develop your capacity for longer periods of focusing your mind exclusively on where you want it to be focused.

- When you complete four consecutive breaths with your mind focused solely on the process of breathing, open your right hand and begin to keep track with your left thumb touching your left index finger. Once you have made four consecutive breaths focusing on only your breathing as measured by your left thumb touching (1) your index finger, (2) your middle finger, (3) your ring finger, and (4) your pinkie, move back to tracking your progress with your right hand, this time skipping your index finger. Touch your thumb to your middle finger, then your ring finger, etc. Then move again to your left hand. If at any time your mind slips away for a significant period of time (and it will), start over with your right thumb on your right index finger.

When other thoughts come to mind as you do this exercise, place them into categories of your choosing. You will begin to see how your mind works and how everything you think tends to fall into only a handful of categories. Let's say you are focusing on your breathing and the following thought comes: "I've got to remember to buy salad today." This is a "To-Do Thought." Silently say, "That is a To-Do Thought," and let the thought go. Catch and categorize your thoughts and then return to focusing only on breathing.

Your mind may begin to dart about like a wild horse, stringing together thoughts such as, "While I'm at the store getting salad, I should also pick up razor blades. . .I wonder why razor blades are so expensive. . .Speaking of money, I wonder how much money I have in my checking account. . .Did I order new checks?"

When this happens, categorize each thought and start over by touching your right thumb to your right index finger.

To control the mind, we must first quiet the mind. The ego knows this and it will do *everything it can* to thwart your efforts. Like a wild horse, the ego wants to show you that it is boss and it will throw whatever it can at you in an attempt to distract you away from meditation.

The Ego Dislikes Meditation

I have been doing this particular meditation daily for almost three years and have discovered that more than 90% of the thoughts that seek my attention while I am meditating fall into just three categories:

1. To-Do Thoughts
2. Self-critical Thoughts
3. Teaching Thoughts

I've discovered that the To-Do Thoughts are often my ego's first attempt to get me to stop meditating and make a list.

When I refuse to comply and stay with my practice, the ego gets personal and begins to say negative and even hurtful things. These Self-critical thoughts are also an attempt to get me to stop meditating and to instead engage in an internal argument defending myself.

When neither of the first two techniques works, my ego tempts me with what I call Teaching Thoughts—ideas that I can develop and share through writing and speaking to help other people. Even these thoughts, beneficial though they may seem, are just decoys to get me to stop meditating.

The ego knows that through meditation we can develop the capacity to send it packing, so it can be relentless and diabolical in its efforts to stop us from this powerful technique to master our inner world.

Just like Monty Roberts drives off a half-ton horse until it is ready to behave, through meditation we can drive off what may seem to be a fierce and enormous ego until it becomes compliant.

Your mind loves to multitask, which is another way of saying "not focus." To sit quietly for an extended period of time and focus only on your breathing takes considerable patience and ongoing practice. The ego will tell you that this is boring and repetitive—and, to be honest, it can be—but that's the point! You are training your mind to do what you want it to do by placing your attention on the common act of breathing, which means you are removing your attention from anything engaging. You are wresting control of your thoughts from your ego. You are pushing your ego into the backseat so you can begin to drive your mind.

Expect resistance when you begin to practice this meditation. The great spiritual master Paramahansa Yogananda wrote, "The soul loves to meditate, for in contact with the Spirit lies its greatest joy. If, then, you experience mental resistance during meditation, remember that reluctance to meditate comes from the ego; it doesn't belong to the soul."

If you can get yourself to stay with this practice on a daily basis and, ideally, expand the length of each meditation to 30 minutes each time, you will begin to experience a newfound power over your thoughts throughout the day. When your ego offers unsolicited comments, you will be able to literally take your mind off what it is saying and keep focus upon what you wish to think about.

It is an incredible feeling when you first dispel the ego in this manner. It's as if you have finally found a "mute" button on your negative inner voice.

You will also discover another wonderful benefit of this practice that will significantly enhance your level of happiness. Because of your repeated practice of taking thoughts and placing them into categories, your overall ability to focus will be enhanced.

For example, imagine that one of your children comes to you and begins to excitedly tell you something that happened at school. In the past, your mind may have begun to drift to something you have to do later, but you have so trained your mind that you now simply categorize the "To-Do Thought" and keep your focus on your precious child.

The Happiness Benefits of Meditation

Beyond the benefits of mastering your mind and learning to categorize your thoughts, the very act of meditating brings increased happiness. Myriad studies have found that meditating releases endorphins into the bloodstream. Endorphins are *endogenous morphine*—powerful drugs produced by your pituitary gland that can significantly elevate your mood.

Your true self—that is, your spirit—is one with all and dwells eternally in the realm of happiness. The spiritual practice of meditation helps you separate from the ego-based human life and live the spiritual life that is your real essence. Author and spiritual teacher Ram Dass put it this way: "Spiritual practices help us move from identifying with the ego to identifying with the soul."

The ego is based in fear. Fear negates happiness. To choose happy thoughts, you must first develop your power to silence the ego and select what you will think. This daily meditation gives you that power.

SEND IN THE CLOWNS

Sometimes it can seem as if other people, especially those closest to you, are intent on finding ways of upsetting you.

We do pretty well maintaining a high degree of happiness until we get around certain people, and then things fall apart. We find ourselves wondering if this person gets up in the morning with the intention of making us unhappy. He or she pushes our buttons and we react and, as a result, our happiness level dips measurably.

To become as happy as you resolve to be requires shifting your thoughts about other people and their antics. To develop this skill, take a lesson from Native Americans.

According to the earliest oral histories, many Native American tribes have had what are commonly referred to as "Sacred Clowns." The Lakota Indians call them *Heyoka*. Among the Pueblo tribes of the Southwest, the Zuni refer to them as Mudheads, and the Hopi call them *Hano*. The Apache call them *Libaye*, and Cheyenne Indians refer to them as Contraries.

Agents of Chaos

A Sacred Clown is a gadfly—a person whose role is to devise and intentionally cause chaos.

Native American scholar Gil Nichols explained the role of the Sacred Clown to me: "The Sacred Clown's job is to jack with people. They literally get up every morning with the intention of warping the experience of other tribal members that day; often by upsetting them. It is their esteemed position in the tribe to do this."

In the sweltering heat of summer, a Sacred Clown might bundle up in heavy winter clothing and complain repeatedly to everyone about the frigid temperature.

If a ceremonial sweat is about to begin and the lodge is already full to capacity, the clown will go about the tribe saying that the sweat lodge is nearly empty and needs more people. Hearing this, Indians hastily pack into the sweat lodge until everyone is jammed in as tight as pickles in a jar.

"Anything they could do to irritate others and thereby shock them out of their complacency is employed," Nichols said.

Even today, when the annual Sun Dance is held in the hallowed Black Hills of South Dakota, Sacred Clowns are present. For four grueling days, dancers perform the steps of their ancestors under a sweltering summer sun without any food or water. Some of the dancers demonstrate their devotion through the ancient ritual of piercing their chests with elk bones and then lashing themselves to a tree with ropes tied to the bone tips protruding from their torn skin.

As a crowd of observers sits in reverential awe at the dancers' devotion, deprivation, and stamina, the Clowns are preparing for their part in the ceremony.

On the third day, when the dancers are exhausted and dehydrated, they question their commitment to this ritual and consider giving up. The Clowns, dressed in black and white, appear with the intention of wreaking havoc. Their coloring, like that of the Chinese yin-yang, symbolizes that darkness exists in all light, and light is present in all darkness.

While the dancers strive to maintain their solemnity and their serenity, the Clowns jump erratically about, taunting them. The Clowns have been known to mount a horse facing backward and ride around the gathering, whooping and calling out to distract the dancers. One year, several Sacred Clowns at one Sun Dance ran through the crowd soaking everyone with giant squirt guns. Anything they can do to create havoc is fair game.

You might think that the Sacred Clowns' irreverent pranks would demoralize and weaken the resolve of the exhausted dancers, who must summon all of their energy and concentration just to continue, but it actually has the opposite effect. A few years ago a Sun Dance was held on the Pine Ridge Reservation, and for the first time, no Sacred Clowns were present. That year, and for the first time ever, several dancers had to be hospitalized due to heat exhaustion. The absence of the Clowns seemed to actually weaken the endurance of the dancers.

In the Beginning, There Was Chaos

Native Americans believe that Sacred Clowns as agents of chaos were the first beings created by the Great Spirit. Chaos was the first thing to be created, because chaos is actually *necessary* for human growth and development. Both Hinduism and Greek mythology share the belief that chaos preceded all other manifestations of creation.

The Sacred Clown is a revered component of a Native American Holy Trinity. The chief is the father, the medicine man is the channel of healing spirit, and the Clown represents the earthly son, who is laughable in his arrogant whims and aspirations.

When we consider the effort it took to simply survive for thousands of years in the harsh outlands of the United States, it is astounding to consider that many Native American tribes designate members whose only purpose is to "jack with the people." More important, it is fascinating that the Clowns' antics are considered both sacred and necessary.

The Gifts of Sacred Clowns

Sacred Clowns serve several purposes:

1. **Keeping people's focus on the present.** The mind tends to wander. But when there is a challenge, the mind snaps back to the here and now so that it can figure out what actions should be taken to resolve an issue.

2. **Challenging and forcing people to clarify their own perspectives and beliefs.** Nothing will help you discover and fully embrace what you believe more than having someone challenge you. In fact, a time-honored tradition for some Buddhist monks is to dispute and argue the basic tenets of Buddhism with apprentice monks. In so doing, the novice is forced to discern the exact meaning of a teaching and more fully make it his own.

3. **Reminding people that challenges are a part of life and a necessary part of growth.** Every day brings its own set of challenges, and the more challenges we successfully overcome, the more we develop the capacity for problem solving. Comedian Christopher Titus, who endured a painful childhood with an abusive alcoholic father and a mother who suffered from mental illness, observed that people who have been through tough times are better able to handle problems, whereas others who have lived more sheltered lives can be traumatized by even minor setbacks and challenges.

4. **Inspiring people to laugh at themselves.** The more spiritual a person becomes, the less little things upset him or her. With this altered perspective, things that once seemed upsetting can be seen as humorous and entertaining rather than distressing.

5. **Helping people stop taking other people's actions personally.** Sacred Clowns continue an ancient practice

of calling forth the demons that fester within the souls of individuals within the tribe. They are attempting to upset people as a way of showing them that they have some previous wounds and triggers to work through.

Historian Gil Nichols explains it this way: "A Sacred Clown reveals you to yourself." When a Sacred Clown upsets you, it is not personal. He or she is simply showing you that your serenity bears further development. "This is why the clowns are referred to as 'sacred,'" says Nichols. "They are doing Spirit's work to clarify and heal the soul."

Wisdom from a Modern-Day Sacred Clown

I spent Thanksgiving 2011 at the Pine Ridge Reservation as the guest of Reed and Anita Brown. Reed and Anita are husband and wife and both are Lakota Sioux. Both are also Sacred Clowns.

Reed is soft-spoken and playful. He is a tall, strong man in his early sixties with mischievous eyes and a face leathered by the sun. The reservation where he lives is the most impoverished region in the United States. The median income in Reed's part of the world is *less than half* of what the US government considers the poverty level, and yet Heyoka Reed seems remarkably tranquil. With all the many challenges he has faced and continues to face, he appears quite happy.

It took awhile for me to get past Reed's tribal trickster persona and to connect with the man behind the Clown. On my second day in the Brown home, I offered Reed a ritual gift of pure tobacco and asked if I might interview him about the role of Sacred Clowns. He looked deep into my eyes as he accepted my gift, indicating that we now had a sacred pact—a three-way agreement between him, the Great Spirit, and me. We had reached an accord to share openly, honestly, and respectfully with one another.

That afternoon we sat and talked as a fire raged before us, heating stones that would later be moved into the sweat lodge to provide heat for the evening's sweat.

As the fire burned down and the sun began to dissolve into the distant horizon, Reed looked out across the prairie and said, "At some point, everyone is a Sacred Clown. Everyone acts a little crazy every now and then, just to bug us and wake us up."

We both sat a moment while I let his comment sink in.

As a coyote wailed in the distance, Reed drew a breath and continued. "White people sit around the dinner table and complain about the unfairness of what happened to them that day. We Indians, on the other hand, have sat together in front of the evening fires for thousands of years sharing and giving thanks for what we learned about ourselves that day as a result of Sacred Clowns taunting us."

We sat quietly as I let Heyoka Reed's comments shine a new light on my relationships with people I find to be difficult and challenging.

"What if these people are simply attempting to wake me up to the hidden areas of my subconscious that need healing?" I wondered. "What if rather than being demons, these people are, in fact, angels, whose divine purpose is to help me become more spiritual?"

Identifying Sacred Clowns

When I returned home, I shared my new understanding with a friend. For more than a decade she had complained to me incessantly about the same coworker. She had said repeatedly that she thought this woman's every action was an intentional attempt to make her life miserable. I explained that perhaps this woman was her Sacred Clown and that if she could begin to view her this way, the things this coworker did would cease to be so upsetting.

"What is it in you that finds her so upsetting?" I asked. "What is being brought up for you to work through, resolve, and heal?"

As my friend considered the wounds that this other woman touched off in her and started to own her upset as her own, she began to experience newfound peace and happiness at work.

To become a happier person, realize that what you find upsetting about other people may actually be something within yourself that needs to be brought up, addressed, and healed. Your greatest tormentors are your mentors. They are your most Sacred Clowns.

Designating problematic people as Sacred Clowns shifts your attitude from condemnation to gratitude. It liberates your mind to feel free and happy.

A friend recently gave me an authentic Native American kachina doll. It has black-and-white horns and stands on one leg as if dancing. In its hands are rattles and on its face is a snarl that seems both playful and threatening. The Sacred Clown doll sits on my desk next to my computer screen, reminding me that when I speak to people, such as customer service reps, and they are not acting in a manner I feel they should, that they are actually my Sacred Clowns attempting to rattle me. My objective is to not react to them but instead to be grateful for them for revealing myself to me and to do my best to keep my happiness at the highest possible level.

Your Internal Heyoka

Before we close this section, I want to leave you with one additional jewel Heyoka Reed shared with me as we talked in front of his sweat lodge. He said, "What white people call the ego is nothing more than an internal Heyoka. It is a Sacred Clown that never goes away but that challenges us at every turn so we can improve and become even more connected with our Great Spirit."

During the western expansion of the 1800s, it was common for the US government to give gifts to Native Americans as bribes for safe passage of settlers. Mirrors were a common trinket offered to Indians, and those typically wound up in the hands of the tribe's Sacred Clowns.

Members of the tribes gave the mirrors they received to their Sacred Clowns for two reasons:

1. The Sacred Clown's role is to reflect back the status of individuals and the tribe as a whole so that areas that needed addressing can be seen clearly.
2. Mirrors reflect back images in reverse. If you write something and hold it up to a mirror, you see it backward. Sacred Clowns often make their points by doing or saying the opposite of what is true.

The ego is a Sacred Clown. All too often we hear it telling us negative things about others and ourselves, and we either accept its statements or argue against them. However, if we remember that the ego is a Heyoka or Contrary *speaking the mirror image of what is true*, we can turn its comments around and find peace and happiness.

If your ego says, "You can't do that," flip it around and say aloud, "You're right, I'll accomplish this easily." If it says, "You're stupid," realize that it is actually stating the mirror image of this comment and say, "Thank you. You're right, I *am* smart."

You have external Sacred Clowns that show up at different times and in various forms as your family, friends, coworkers, other drivers on the highway, and even people you meet only in passing. You also have an internal Sacred Clown (your ego) that will perpetually try to rattle you. You will find that the more you meditate and work with your internal Sacred Clown, giving it an easily dismissible voice and flipping its comments around, the fewer external Sacred Clowns you will encounter.

IT'S ONLY A GAME

Last year while I was on a speaking tour in Asia, I was constantly recharging my smartphone—but not because I was engaged in important telephone calls, doing research, or sending emails.

No, there was a plague that had swept the world, and I was hopelessly infected by it. Whenever there was a spare moment, I anxiously sought out my phone and furiously tapped the screen.

While I was in cabs, on planes, even when I was eating alone at restaurants, I was using my phone to scratch the itch of the obsession I was caught up in, along with more than 11 million people around the world—a new smartphone game. When a friend first told me about it, I thought it sounded like a silly concept; but when I actually downloaded the game and tried it, I was utterly hooked.

In case you haven't guessed by now, the game is Angry Birds.

The Lure of Higher Levels

It seems so simple—pull back a slingshot and launch one of a variety of cartoon birds at leering green cartoon pigs. After one launches the app, the Angry Birds welcome screen comes up and the player is presented with a grid of squares, each representing a level of play. The player can select to replay any previous level; but the player cannot proceed to a higher level until the current level is successfully completed.

When I first arrived in China on the first leg of my tour, I mindlessly played the game while waiting to move through customs. I completed level after level, but then something both terrible and exciting happened. I reached level 12, and I absolutely could not figure out how to clear out all the little pigs with my allotted birds.

I tried everything I remembered from previous levels, and nothing seemed to work. The game went from being an idle pastime to a relentless obsession. Even when I was not playing, my mind was attempting to figure out what I needed to do to complete level 12.

Surpassing level 12 became my all-consuming goal. As my speaking tour drew to a close, I lay in my hotel bed late one night—later than I'd like to admit—frantically playing Angry Birds, trying in vain to overcome level 12.

I repeated a maneuver I had tried hundreds of times previously, but the angle or my release of the slingshot must have been just slightly different and the last little green pig on the screen popped like a balloon.

"I did it!" I yelled into the empty room. "I finally did it!" I was so excited I considered calling friends and family members back home in the United States. I even thought about getting dressed and going through the hotel knocking randomly on doors, telling everyone, "I finally completed level 12 on Angry Birds!"

I wisely realized that if I did this people might question my sanity, so I placed my phone into its charger and rolled over to go to sleep, basking in the glow of my triumph.

Now, what do you think I did when I awoke the following morning?

You're right; I instinctively reached for my phone. As the Angry Birds welcome screen faded away and I saw the levels that

I could revisit, I looked with arrogant disdain at the button for level 12. I now knew the secret to defeating this level and could do it at will.

I restarted level 12, which for nearly two weeks had seemed insurmountable and defeated it in less than a minute. Once more I launched 12 and easily completed it again.

When the game asked what level I wanted to play next, rather than selecting a level from 1 to 12 that I had completed and could easily defeat, I selected level 13 and my obsession and enthusiasm began anew.

The Game of Life

Later that day, as I was strolling along the riverfront near my hotel, I thought about my manic obsession with this game. More important, I wondered to myself why I had gained so much enjoyment from trying to complete a level that was difficult, but found little or no satisfaction in easily winning at a level I had already mastered.

When I was trying to conquer a new and more difficult level, I was excited, engaged, and eager. Even when I struggled with the challenge, I was happy. I was content. However, when I replayed a previous level that no longer offered any challenge, I was discontented.

I realized that this is the nature of life. People tend to have a false belief that they would like to never face another challenge, and yet much of our happiness comes in facing and overcoming challenges.

Even though this book was well outlined long before I began writing, each day I stare at a blinking cursor that seems to taunt me, saying "OK, so far, so good, but what's next?" In the writing of this book, I feel happy because I have a high degree of enthusiasm mixed with an equal measure of uncertainty.

As I complete chapter after chapter, I find satisfaction in my work. Each new chapter provides an opportunity for me to stare down the cursor and get typing, so that as I lie in bed at night, I feel good about my writing for that day. I feel content. And remember that our definition for happiness is more like contentment than joy.

Striving for Happiness

My brother Dave says his sole desire during his working life has been to "make enough money so I can lie on a beach and do nothing for the rest of my life." He is a very talented and successful man. Thus far, his dream of becoming rich so he can live out the remainder of his days as a piece of human driftwood has eluded him, and I hope that it always will.

Whenever we talk, he tells me with great enthusiasm about some new challenge he is facing. He thinks his life would be better and he would be happier if he no longer had such challenges to overcome. However, if he were to become a person of total leisure, he would lose the divine spark that brings him such enthusiasm and joy and that squeezes out every drop of his creativity, allowing him to discover just how talented and capable he truly is.

Earl Nightingale, who has been called the "Dean of the School of Motivation," noted that a dog chasing a rabbit is much happier than a dog lying on a porch. And that is why, regardless of our level of income and success, we desire more. Getting more means giving more. Giving more means discovering more to give.

It is the act of striving for something that makes us happy, because we are engaged and discovering more of what lies within us. It is not catching the rabbit that makes us happy, but the thrill of the chase. And this explains why most wealthy people who cease to find new ideas to apply and new challenges to overcome tend to feel less happy and less satisfied.

In *The Big Leap*, Gay Hendricks writes that each of us has what he calls a "Zone of Genius," a realm of activity that pulls our talents and abilities to the forefront of our lives. Hendricks notes that most people spend their lives in what he calls a "Zone of Excellence"—an arena that satisfies others and in which we shine, but which never completely snaps us into the fullness of who we are. Happiness is found in the Zone of Genius.

As a friend of mine recently put it, "Happiness is a job that connects all of my dots." That is, a career path that fully utilizes all of our skills and talents.

When I think of the word "genius," Apple Computer founder Steve Jobs immediately comes to mind. I read a biography of Jobs decades ago and was impressed that no matter how much money he had, he was always trying to figure out new and better ways to positively integrate technology into people's lives. Certainly, he made a lot of money in the process, but the subtitle of the book I had read, *The Journey Is the Reward,* spoke to a higher purpose in his work.

Jobs could have quit work, bought his own island, and plopped on the beach decades ago, but he remained engaged in his life and his work right up until the end, and the world is a better place for it. And so, too, was his life!

Maintaining Enthusiasm

The word "enthusiasm" comes from the Greek *entheos*, which means "the God within." Facing new levels of difficulty calls forth the divine within us, and we get to surprise and delight ourselves in discovering and observing skills and aptitudes that previously lay dormant.

Happiness doesn't come from avoiding challenges. It comes from facing and overcoming challenges. One of the keys to having happy thoughts is to release the belief that life will one day fall into place and cease to present difficulties. Happiness comes from getting up every morning looking forward to discovering how gifted we are through the overcoming of our challenges and then lying in bed at night satisfied for having given our best.

Happy people choose to view life's difficulties very differently from unhappy people.

Unhappy people think that difficulties are the universe picking on them. They think that they will be happy if and when all of life's problems cease. Of course, this never happens, and so they push happiness away.

Happy people use their thoughts to reframe difficulties into challenges. They seek out what they can learn in difficult situations and how they can grow through them.

In Chapter 2, I shared that Arnold Schwarzenegger clearly defined the body he wished to have and, as a result, won six consecutive Mr. Olympia titles, which was a world record at the time.

Bodybuilding is a sport that requires an athlete to repeatedly challenge the body in order to grow. Heavier amounts of weight and/or more repetitions force muscles beyond their current capacity, and the muscles rebuild larger and stronger.

Your soul's desire is to grow, and so it presents you with opportunities—yes, *opportunities* called challenges—so you can overcome them. As you face them one by one, you find that you become stronger. You then go on to new and greater challenges. Facing the same issue over and over would be no more challenging, interesting, or rewarding than playing a previous level on a video game. As psychiatrist Theodore I. Rubin said, "Happiness does not come from doing easy work but from the afterglow of satisfaction that comes after the achievement of a difficult task that demanded our best."

Life Is Constructed in order to Bring You Happiness

Every day brings new challenges, right? You experience happiness when you overcome challenges, correct? Therefore, if you shift your thinking and begin to anticipate challenges so that you can "show your stuff," you can enjoy the game of life and its ever-challenging levels.

When a difficulty pops up, think, "I can't wait to see how I'll handle this!" In other words, don't get upset because you have a new challenge; accept that this is just the process of moving from level to level and it is the natural course of living. If you take a moment to look back on your life, you will see that this is the way it has always been, so you can assume that life will always be this way and you might as well enjoy the process.

To become a truly happy person, you must begin to control your thoughts—notice I said "*your* thoughts" because they are yours. No one can control your thoughts except you.

Your mind is the epicenter of your life. Everything starts with your thinking, which sends shock waves out into what you call reality.

In her book *The How of Happiness*, psychologist Sonja Lyubomirsky writes, "It is a truism that how you think about yourself, your world and other people is more important to your happiness than the objective circumstances of your life."

RECAPPING "THOUGHTS OF HAPPINESS"

- When you think you are happy, you are happy.

- When you separate your thoughts from your ego, you liberate yourself to be happy.

- When you take control of your thinking, you can choose to think happy thoughts.

- When you cease to rail against other people and begin to think of them as Sacred Clowns, you release resentment and find happiness.

- When you accept that you will always have challenges and that they exist to keep you actively engaged and growing, you have found the first step to sustainable higher levels of happiness.

CHAPTER FOUR

Words of Happiness

> *All our words are but crumbs that fall down from the feast of the mind.*
> —Khalil Gibran

You cannot have a word without first having a thought. Words are thoughts that vibrate out into the world—literally.

Consider the process of speaking. You have a thought you choose to articulate and so you pass air across your vocal cords, causing them to vibrate. The vibration of your vocal cords creates sound in a tone and frequency that matches your thought in the form of words. This energy is projected out and received by others. They, in turn, respond to and reflect back what you have said.

Thoughts precede words, but what you may not realize is that it is a two-way process. You observe how what you have spoken is received, noting other people's comments and facial expressions.

This can impact your thinking, which in turn can shift the words you speak. It's an instantaneous and ongoing process:

Thoughts > Words > Reactions & Responses >
Thoughts > Words. . .Etc.

Once you begin to think like a happy person, you will automatically change the way you speak and how you describe your experiences. You will begin to use words that reflect greater levels of enjoyment, compassion, and appreciation, and at the same time you will cease to complain and commiserate. Your mind now vibrates at a higher level and your words reflect your happier thoughts.

However, as you begin this transformation, you can expect some people to feel uncomfortable with your metamorphosis. You may experience obstacles in the form of the reactions and responses from other people that make you uncomfortable.

Once again, to equate happiness to fitness, people are as fit as they choose to be and they are as happy as they choose to be. Because being fit and being happy take a willingness to put forth effort, many people ignore both their fitness and their happiness levels. Unfortunately, these same people can then feel threatened by anyone who dares to break out and become either happy or fit, because it magnifies their lack of effort by comparison.

Envy creates a feeling of inferiority, and it is the nature of inferiority to attack that which it perceives to be superior. As you become happier, people who are unwilling to put forth the effort to be happy feel a compelling need to narrow the perceived gap between you and them. They have two choices: become happier, or do whatever they can to bring you down to their level.

The tendency to criticize people to whom we feel inferior was made famous in the Lee Ann Womack song "I'll Think of a

Reason Later." The character in this popular song says she hates another woman who she sees in her local newspaper's wedding announcements. Regardless of the woman's many positive attributes, she says that she hates her anyway—obviously, out of jealousy—and will think of a reason why she hates her later.

Envy is a powerful drug. It is an anesthetic that numbs the pain of embarrassment. Envy explains the dozens of "celebrity" magazines we see as we check out at the grocery store. In a recent interview on NPR's *Fresh Air*, the great actor Sir Ben Kingsley was asked his opinion of celebrity magazines. He responded that this genre of magazines is misnamed. "They're not 'celebrity' magazines," he said. "They don't celebrate. They attack."

Attacking people who we feel make us look bad by comparison takes the focus off of our own lack of effort and rationalizes lower levels of achievement.

As you become happier, you may find that some people may not be supportive of this important positive shift in your life. People who are less happy tend to put down happy people by dismissing them as naive, out of touch, or even phony.

In addition, some people in your life may initially support your quest for happiness but then attempt to sabotage your efforts. This is because a happy person is difficult to control and, unfortunately, some relationships are all about control.

The chances are good that Sacred Clowns such as these will show up to discourage you. This is why it is a good idea to have a Happiness Buddy to support and offer regular encouragement.

Be vigilant and strengthen your resolve to stay on course to live at a happier level. Eventually, your detractors will not only stop trying to discourage you; those very same people will probably begin to emulate you and become happier themselves. Mahatma Gandhi is said to have explained this proclivity of people to attack others who are seeking to bring about positive change: "First they ignore you, then they laugh at you, then they fight you, then you win."

If someone gives you static for desiring to become happier, marvel at what a wonderful job this Sacred Clown is doing by taunting you, thereby inspiring you to strengthen your resolve and win.

The famed British journalist Holbrook Jackson had it right when he said, "Happiness is a form of courage." To reach and maintain higher and happier levels, you must begin to consistently project yourself out into the world as a happy person.

ABRACADABRA!

The phrase "idle talk" is an oxymoron.

Talk is never idle. Talk proclaims to ourselves and to others what we are thinking, and our thoughts create our lives. Speaking in positive ways and eliminating negative statements makes you feel happier.

This has been proven by a great many people who have taken the Complaint Free Challenge. The program began in 2006 when I encouraged people to strive to go 21 consecutive days without complaining. The idea exploded around the world and, as of this writing, more than 10 million people in 106 countries have taken up the challenge. You can find out more at AComplaintFreeWorld.org.

The most frequent comment I have received from people who have undertaken the Complaint Free Challenge is that they feel happier. When people cease to gripe about other people and challenging situations, their levels of happiness increase of their own accord.

What this demonstrates is that although your words are sourced by your thoughts, your thoughts are impacted by your words. Intentionally driving your words from the negative lane into the positive lane simultaneously takes your thoughts along for the ride. Happy thoughts lead to happy words, but happy words also inspire happier thoughts, and both generate a higher level of happiness.

Stage magicians often speak incantations as part of their acts. They will shout so-called magic words such as "Abracadabra!" Most people believe "Abracadabra!" is just gibberish like "Hocus-pocus!" or "Presto change-o!" However, "abracadabra" is a true magic word.

The word is thought to have its origin in the Aramaic language. It is a combination of *ibra*, which means "I have created," and *k'dibra*, meaning "through my speech." "Abracadabra," therefore, means "I have created through the power of my speech!" There is magic in what we say because it creates our reality.

Nobel Prize–winning Jewish-American author Isaac Bashevis Singer said, "If you keep on saying things are going to be bad, you have a good chance of becoming a prophet." Of course, this works both ways. If you keep on saying things are going to be good, they will tend to be good, which provides more to be happy about.

Life is a tuning fork. It responds to the energy of your thoughts. When you speak, you concretize your thoughts into reality. Changing what you say changes your experience.

Happy people are very careful not to say things that will stir up negative emotions in themselves or negativity in others, because that energy will come back to them. Other people, as well as life itself, respond to what you say. The Buddha said, "Do not speak harshly to anyone; those who are spoken to will answer thee in the same way." The same is true of life; harsh words create a harsh reality, and it is difficult to maintain a high level of happiness living in a harsh reality.

Unhappy people and happy people speak quite differently about their lives and, as a result, they experience vastly different realities.

> *Unhappy people speak of weighty problems.*
> *Happy people speak of exciting challenges.*

> *Unhappy people say that no amount of*
> *effort will make a difference.*
> *Happy people express faith that an*
> *optimal outcome is possible.*

> *Unhappy people speak of another person's rudeness.*
> *Happy people speak compassionately of the*
> *challenges a person must have experienced*
> *to result in his or her rude behavior.*

> *Unhappy people are affronted by the actions of other people.*
> *Happy people give thanks for the lessons they learn*
> *from the Sacred Clowns that show up in their lives.*

Begin to speak in positive ways about your life. Rather than speaking negatively about your perceived shortcomings and those you see in others, talk about what you find favorable or *don't talk at all*!

The Myth of Venting

Venting about your life and your experiences does not make you happier. This is a myth. If venting about your problems made you happier, then the biggest complainers would be the happiest people—and we all know this is not true. Complaining is a low-vibration form of communication that makes you feel less happy.

When you complain about something, you are putting your focus upon what is wrong rather than speaking about how you would like things to be and—"Abracadabra!"—you cause this negative experience to continue, through the power of your words.

Speaking negatively is a habit that can be broken through repetition. As often as possible, reframe what you say from negative to positive. Catch yourself when you express a complaint. Say "Abracadabra!" and realize that you have just increased the likelihood of this issue continuing. Then, reframe the situation to what you would like the outcome to be and say, again, "Abracadabra!"

Begin to think of all of your words as magic words. What you say is magic because it creates either the illusion that your life is enjoyable or that your life is miserable.

Emily Dickinson wrote a poem about the creative power of words:

> *A word is dead*
> *When it is said,*
> *Some say.*
> *I say it just*
> *Begins to live*
> *That day.*

Your words come alive as your life when you speak them. Carefully select what you say, because you will become what you speak.

"Abracadabra!"

TELL ME A STORY

How you phrase your experience frames your life.

We live in a neutral world, which we then charge with the energy of our thoughts and our words. We attempt to give meaning to our experiences by creating stories about anything and everything. With the power of our words we set the context of life, and this sets off a vibration within our minds that resonates with the story we have created. We then look out into our circumstances and seek validation for our story; by seeking it out we often find it.

My daughter, Lia, now 16, is dating a young man from another school. Although they don't get to see one another often, they constantly stay in touch, texting throughout the day.

One afternoon, I asked Lia how her boyfriend was doing and she said, "I don't know, I haven't heard from him in a day or so."

"Haven't heard from him in a day or so? That's odd," I thought.

Lia continued to text her boyfriend several times a day and to call him periodically, but did not receive a response. During lunch at school, she told her friends about her boyfriend's lack of response to her texts and calls. A few of them drew heavy sighs and looked at her with deep concern.

"You know what that means, right?" said one.

"No," answered Lia. "What does it mean?"

The girl shifted uncomfortably in her seat and then sent a knowing glance to the other girls around the table. "It means you've broken up," she said.

"What do you mean we've broken up?" Lia asked with a bemused smile.

As if explaining the painfully obvious, the girl leaned forward and whispered, "Lia, you guys text and talk all the time. If he has suddenly gone into silent mode, it means that he doesn't want to be your boyfriend anymore and he doesn't have the guts to come out and tell you."

Lia looked around the table into the faces of the other girls, several of whom were nodding in agreement.

"Or. . ." Lia said brightly, "or, it could be that he lost his phone."

The other girls' compassionate looks began to fade into slow disbelieving shakes of the head.

Lia was undaunted.

"Or. . ." she said even more confidently, "his phone is broken. Or, he lost his charger. . ."

The looks shifted to pity.

"Or. . ." Lia said smilingly, "his parents took away his phone privileges."

None of the girls accepted this or any of Lia's other possible stories as to why she had not heard from her boyfriend. With a sneer, one of the girls gathered the trash from her lunch and stood up mumbling, "Whatever gets you through the night, Lia." She tossed in one of those patented teenage girl back-and-forth head movements for emphasis.

That evening, Lia related the lunch conversation to me and said that she still hadn't heard from her guy.

I have to admit, I felt a growing hole in my heart. As a young man, I had a couple of girlfriends who seemed to be very much into me but then suddenly changed their minds. I remembered the sting of their rejection. As much as I know my daughter is going to experience her own setbacks, challenges, and even heartbreaks, I would love to somehow find a way to shield her from pain.

"What do you think the real story is?" I asked with a gentle smile.

"I really don't know," she said. "But I know he likes me, so I'm guessing his phone is lost or broken or his parents took his phone from him."

I did my best to join her in believing one of these scenarios and let it go.

A few days later I asked, "Have you heard from your boyfriend?"

"Yep," Lia said. "He called last night. He finally got his phone privileges back. His parents had taken his phone away because his grades had slipped."

For a period of five days, she had not heard from him, and yet Lia's level of happiness never dipped. During this time she did not know the true story as to why he had not responded to her calls and texts, but she chose to tell herself stories that supported their relationship being happy and strong. As I write this, they are still together after six months—which, by teenage standards, is a serious long-term relationship.

Why This Can Be Difficult

If you find it difficult to frame unknowable situations into positive stories, there is a reason for this. Studies have found that when we worry about a situation and it comes to pass, our level of upset is diminished, because we have prepared ourselves for the possibility of things going badly.

However, the amount of diminished grief we feel is small compared to the cumulative pain of fear, anxiety, and worry we string together over days, weeks, or even months of fretting about what might happen.

Further, and most important, because our lives reflect our thoughts, if we tell ourselves negative stories as to what might transpire, we are far more likely for this to become our reality.

What if Lia had been wrong? What if her boyfriend *had* decided to break up with her and was too cowardly to tell her? When she finally found out, this would have caused her pain. But thanks to the story she chose to tell, she negated nearly a week of worry and fear. Had they actually split up, she would have only had to deal with that pain rather than the sleepless nights of worry that led up to the breakup.

You cannot be worried and be happy at the same time.

Try it: Think about something you worry about and also try to feel happy. You can't do it. It's like trying to smell the delicious aroma of a pie baking in the oven while having two sweaty gym socks shoved in your nostrils. It simply can't be done.

Preview of Coming Attractions

The English word "worry" comes from the Proto-Indo-European word *wring*, as in to wring someone's neck, or strangle. Worry strangles our capacity to feel happiness, and the stories that we tell others and ourselves either increase or decrease worry. They are never neutral.

Albert Einstein said, "Imagination is everything. It is the preview of life's coming attractions." What you imagine in your mind becomes the trailer for the movie that is your upcoming future. Ask yourself these questions:

- Is my preview of coming attractions a love story or a tale of heartbreak?
- Is my life's movie trailer about a comedy or a tragedy?

- Does my preview foretell a hero's triumphant victory or a painful defeat?

Then, go back into the editing room of your mind and splice together the preview you want and begin to talk about this story to yourself and others.

Trailers, just like the movies they synopsize, have ratings such as G, PG, PG-13, etc. Don't stop re-editing your trailer until you can give it an A for "awesome."

It's All in How You Explain It

Martin Seligman, the founder of positive psychology, discovered that happy people are distinguished from unhappy people by what he calls their "explanatory style." Happy people tend to explain things to themselves and others in ways that make them feel good, whereas unhappy people tend to explain things in ways that make them feel bad. The perspective people choose to adopt when telling a story is the single greatest determinant of their level of happiness.

Get creative with your stories. Err on the side of awesome! A character in J. D. Salinger's book *Raise High the Roof Beam, Carpenters* puts it perfectly when he says, "I'm a kind of paranoiac in reverse. I suspect people of plotting to make me happy." Develop the same habit. Tell stories of how great things are and how much better they will be in the future.

Practice telling positive stories to yourself. Talk to yourself when you are in the shower, driving, walking, or anytime you are alone. Begin to speak words of great and miraculous experiences yet to come. Use the power of your words to put out into the world the energy of your belief so that you get to hear what you are saying.

I recently learned that Abraham Lincoln read aloud anything that was of importance. Today, we would understand that Lincoln had an auditory learning style. New research finds that this skill helped him stay focused on his objectives, allowing him to get the Emancipation Proclamation passed.

When you speak happy ideas and describe wonderful scenarios aloud, you get to hear yourself affirming them and you take them in even more deeply, inspiring your mind to even happier thoughts. Further, and most important, you begin to look for supporting evidence for your stories and you find it everywhere.

CONTEMPLATION FROM THE HIGHEST POINT OF VIEW

The most powerful words you can use are words of affirmative prayer.

Rather than rambling off a list of requests for God to fulfill, affirmative prayer is declaring that there is much to be happy about in your life and attuning yourself to this reality.

Remember that your mind hears every word you speak and that your mind is the ignition spark for your experience.

Ralph Waldo Emerson said, "Prayer is the contemplation of the facts of life from the highest point of view." Prayer is affirming a divine presence in whatever we are going through and, as a result, finding the comfort, inspiration, and peace of that presence.

Just as Lia told herself and her friends an optimal story regarding her relationship, we should talk to God about an optimal version of our lives through prayer.

Danish philosopher Søren Kierkegaard said, "Prayer does not change God, but changes him who prays." Speaking words that affirm optimal outcomes creates an environment of hope. It eradicates the grip of fear and worry and happiness, then gushes forth like a spring torrent.

I had a conversation with my friend Lama Chuck Stanford of the Rime Buddhist Center in Kansas City regarding prayer from a Buddhist perspective. His summation of Buddhist prayer parallels Kierkegaard's words. Lama Chuck said, "Prayer is about transforming your own mind."

God doesn't need your prayers—you do. Prayer affirms a higher presence in every situation and it confirms your ability to commune and tap into that presence.

To increase your happiness level, pray early and pray often.

The ACT of Prayer

Praying makes you happier not because God is appeased by your offering and then imbues you with happiness. Rather, prayer deepens your connection to spirit and raises your perspective of life to a higher level. You begin to see things from the highest point of view, giving you a sense of comfort and contentment.

Gandhi said, "Prayer is not an old woman's idle amusement. Properly understood and applied, it is the most potent instrument of action."

Many of us are taught as young children to pray by asking God for this and that. As a result, this concept of affirmative prayer may feel foreign or even awkward. Remember Gandhi's comment that prayer is an instrument of *action* and let your prayers follow the simple acronym **ACT**.

Acknowledge the Presence of the Divine

This can be done simply by saying "God, I know you are present in this situation." Or, "Sacred Spirit, I know that you are one with me." Or, "Infinite love, you are in the midst of this."

The words are not important. What is important is to acknowledge that God is present. When we are experiencing a difficult challenge, it can be a struggle to do this. To the extent that we feel God is not present, we limit our connection to God. Affirmative prayer means we first affirm that God is, indeed, in the house.

To remember this truth, I have a bronze plaque on my wall bearing a Latin motto popularized by psychiatrist Carl Jung. It reads "Vocatus atque non vocatus, Deus aderit," which translates to "Bidden or unbidden, God is always present."

Affirming the presence of the divine is not about calling in God. It's about shifting your mind to the understanding that you are currently immersed in the fullness of all that is sacred.

Claim a Positive Outcome

In *The "I AM" Discourses*, spiritual leader Saint Germain states, "I say to the students in all sincerity, there is no possible way of attaining a quality or a desired attribute without claiming it."

To pray affirmatively is to state an ideal outcome and to claim it as being present now. What you seek already exists as a metaphysical reality. When you claim it *now*, you move it from the realm of the metaphysical into the physical. It already exists in the universal inventory; claiming what you desire moves it into your shopping cart.

"Claiming what you desire" may sound arrogant, but remember that Jesus said, "As you believe so shall it be done unto you" (Matthew 8:13). The word "belief" is defined as "something you have decided to be true." Claiming a positive outcome is stating that what you desire is true; this is the essence of belief, and belief is the catalyst for all manifestation.

It is important that the positive outcome you claim not be off somewhere in the future. In Spirit, there *is* no future; there is only now. Instead of saying "I see myself someday employed," say "I am employed now in a job I love."

The more specific you can be with your outcome, the better. Here is an example of acknowledging the presence of God and then claiming a specific positive outcome:

"Divine Love, I know that you are active in my healing. I feel my body free of pain. Both of my hips feel comfortable and I walk unassisted. I can climb the stairs into my home without the use of the handrail. I am able to rise from the couch without pushing up with my hands, and I feel great."

The more detail you add, the more real your claim becomes for you. And the more real it is, the more you activate the power of belief.

Here are some other examples of claiming a positive outcome:

- *I see myself enjoying a great relationship with my son.*
- *I am in a job that I enjoy, and I earn $56,000 per year.*
- *I feel even happier today than I did yesterday.*
- *I have an intimate partner who adores me.*

State your claim and then give it as complete a description as you can.

Your ego will probably feel threatened and may challenge your belief by continually demanding to know *how* what you are claiming will come to pass. To quote my good friend Joe Vitale, "*How* is the purview of the universe!" Claim what you desire and it will become real in your life; leave the details to God.

Give Thanks

In *Wishes Fulfilled*, Wayne Dyer quotes Neville, "Whether we see immediate results or not, our thanks acknowledge that somewhere in creation our prayer has already been fulfilled."

Conclude your affirmative prayers by expressing thanks. The power of closing your prayers with thanks is that it amplifies the power of your belief.

Here's why: If I handed you a gift, you would say "Thank you." Why? Because you have the gift in your possession. I have given the gift to you and you are grateful for receiving it, so you express your gratitude.

If, however, I said that I might someday give you a gift, you may not choose to thank me, because the gift is only a vague and distant possibility.

Giving thanks reaffirms your claim that what we desire is present now. When you say thank you it is a testament to your faith that what you desire is already yours and by divine right it must show up.

If you were to ask a friend to do you a favor and she said she would, you would say thanks. Not because the favor had been done but because you have certainty that your friend is reliable and will do it. Gratitude expresses certainty, and certainty is the very definition of faith.

Using the power of your words to Acknowledge the Presence of the Divine, Claim a Positive Outcome, and Give Thanks eradicates fear and worry, thereby allowing you to maintain a higher level of happiness.

CHOOSE THE "I AM" CHANNEL

When I speak, I'll often ask my audience, "Who is the greatest boxer of all time?"

Without exception, more than 90% of the crowd will shout back, "Muhammad Ali!"

If Ali was your answer, I've got some sobering news for you. Based on objective criteria such as numbers of fights in various weight classes and the number of championship belts won, the greatest boxer of all time is actually Roy Jones, Jr.

Why, then, do most people consider Muhammad Ali to be the greatest? Who says Ali is the greatest? Who started this rumor?

The answer to all of these questions is the same: Ali!

Most people think Ali was the greatest because he told everyone he is the greatest. Who says Ali is the greatest? He did. Who started this rumor? Ali did.

And the rumor of his absolute superiority in boxing continues to this day. In fact, if you do a Google search asking, "What was Muhammad Ali's nickname as a boxer?" The answer comes back, "The Greatest!"

Wow, no wonder this idea continues.

I remember years ago being in my mother's station wagon as she carpooled several kids and me to school. My mom had the radio on. The station's sports report aired, and that morning I heard the voice of Muhammad Ali for the first time.

The reporter asked Ali about his upcoming fight with Joe Frazier. Ali responded that he would win decisively.

"How do you know for sure?" asked the interviewer.

Rather than discuss his training or his skills as a boxer, Ali said without a shred of doubt, "Because, I am the *greatest!*"

"Yes, but—" blurted the reporter,

"*I* am the greatest!" Ali repeated.

"But Frazier—" interjected the sportscaster.

"I *am* the greatest!" said Ali.

"Yes, but Frazier has said that he—"

"I am *the* greatest!" said Ali yet again.

The reporter signed off the segment as Ali in the background repeated the sentence, each time stressing a different word, "*I* am the greatest! I *am* the greatest! I am *the* greatest! I am the *greatest!*"

My mother clicked her tongue and switched off the radio. "That man sure *loves* himself," she said, as if she had just paid Ali the worst possible criticism. I nodded my head in agreement, and several of my friends nodded their heads as well.

My mother's comment seeped into my head, leaving me with a belief that to claim that I am in any way special, good, or competent is somehow a negative trait. To say that you are good is, we discovered, definitely bad.

Egotism

Many people have been taught that to speak well of themselves is the mark of an ego that is out of control. By now I hope you realize that the ego tends to work exactly the opposite way. The ego puts us down; it does not build us up.

When the ego has sufficiently diminished a person's self-worth, he or she may then become arrogant or boastful in an attempt to prove to others that he or she is not as bad as the ego has convinced this person to believe. But this is the mark of inferiority, not superiority.

In *The Lazy Man's Guide to Enlightenment,* Thaddeus Golas explains, "Loving yourself is not a matter of building your ego. Egotism is proving you are worthwhile after you have sunk into hating yourself. Loving yourself will dissolve your ego: you will feel no need to prove you are superior."

Muhammad Ali wasn't boasting, he was affirming. He was in a brutal and highly competitive sport and if he didn't believe he was the best, there was no way he could succeed. In many ways, Ali's confident statements about his ability were activating the work of Sacred Clowns in the form of sportswriters, other boxers, and the general public. Their attacks on him made Ali all the more committed to prove that he was the greatest. Ali stepped into the fire of public scrutiny, and nothing makes you dance like having your feet in the fire.

Ali had to first convince himself that he deserved to win. And, why did he deserve to win? Because he was the greatest!

You have committed to being happier, but it is difficult to feel happy if you don't feel you deserve to be happy. Unfortunately, most of us have remnants of self-doubt and insecurity that have tattered the edges of the fabric of our lives.

Overcoming Unworthiness

In *Conquer Your Critical Inner Voice*, the authors explain what they refer to as the "fantasy bond." When a child is very young, his or her parents provide everything for the child. Parents are the source of the child's welfare and safety.

Because of their all-powerful role in the child's life, parents are seen to be God in the innocent and immature minds of a child.

The child is too young to comprehend that his or her parents are just human beings with very human faults, shortcoming, and difficulties. So, if one or both parents act in an unloving, harsh, or critical way toward the child, the child is left with a dilemma.

For the child to feel safe and have a sense of hope, God must be infallible. God can never be wrong. If God (in the child's view, his or her parents) treats the child as unlovable, God cannot be wrong; therefore, the child reasons that he or she must not deserve to be loved. This becomes a core belief for the child, and the authors of *Conquer Your Critical Inner Voice* explain that the child then seeks external verification of this core belief.

In psychology, this is known as the "self-verification theory." The child will act in ways that prove that he or she is bad and unlovable. He or she does this in an unrealized attempt to validate the infallibility of the parents who represent God. As a result of the child's actions, other children and even adults will pick up on this belief and treat the child as bad and unlovable. This reinforces the core belief, which perpetuates the behavior.

This feeling of being unlovable becomes a self-fulfilling prophecy that continues into adulthood, manifesting itself in business failures, broken relationships, and poor health. The child, now an adult, feels resentful and angry and, as a result, experiences lower levels of happiness!

Parents love their children. Why then would they treat them as unlovable? Because some parents were themselves treated as unlovable by their own parents—who were treated that way by *their* parents. People who were treated as bad and unlovable when they were children harbor a latent belief that any child that comes through them must be as flawed as they believe themselves to be.

I struggled with my self-worth for many years until I realized that I was caught in this fantasy bond. It was the single greatest block to my happiness because I felt at my core that I did not deserve to be happy. I believed that I deserved problems and people treating me harshly and, as a result, I lived in a problematic and cruel world. Every time I got close to breaking through to a sustained level of happiness, I would do something to mess things up, because I was bound to my belief, even though I was unaware I held this belief.

When I learned about the fantasy bond, I could see it at work in my own childhood and perpetuating itself into my adulthood. Specifically, I could see how my father's acting angry and unloving toward me during my formative years caused me to resign myself to believing I deserved such treatment.

Today, my father is the sweetest and most loving man I know. At 82 years of age, he never ends a phone conversation without telling me he loves me. He sends me emails to tell me he is proud of me. He is more than my father; he is my friend.

If this is the case, why did I struggle with insecurity and unworthiness? Because the man he is today is not the man he was when I was a boy. My thoughts that I was a bad person—and the subsequent pattern this belief created—were reinforced thousands of times throughout my life by my own beliefs.

My dad and I have talked at length about my childhood as well as his own. I may have had it tough, but his childhood was a horror story by comparison. I have dedicated this book to him because of the emotional work he has done to move from being a tortured soul into being a loving man. His metamorphosis has been long and painful, but he stands as a testament to the triumph of love and perseverance over adversity.

To Be Happy, You Must Believe You Deserve Happiness

Happiness is your birthright. It is your destiny. It is the meaning and purpose of life. You are lovable and worthy of happiness.

To know that you deserve to be happy, first understand that you may be carrying around a false belief that you are not worthy or lovable. Acknowledge this belief and understand that your parents are, like you, just people, who often fall short of the ideal.

Their inability to give you the unconditional love you deserve is *not* a reflection on you.

At this realization I have seen some people fall into a trap of logic. Beware of the snare that follows this line of thinking:

- *I'm bad; I'm unlovable.*
- *Wait! It's not that I'm bad; it's not that I'm unlovable, it's that my parents weren't loving.*
- *I'm not bad; they are bad for not loving me!*
- *They are bad, but I'm their child.*
- *Therefore, as their child, I must also be bad.*

Understanding the fantasy bond is realizing why you carry around the erroneous belief that you are unworthy. It is not about placing blame. Shifting blame from yourself onto your parents only places it squarely back on your own shoulders.

Forget blame—that is the ego's attempt to distract you from transformation. Just understand that you are probably carrying around some degree of a core belief that you are not good enough, and this has caused life to mirror back and reinforce this idea.

Changing Your Core Belief

We are going to use the power of words to shift your belief about yourself, creating fertile ground for happiness to take root and grow. We are going to help you override the recordings that run in your mind so that you can realize and live as the truly lovable person you are.

Scientists believe that you think approximately 70,000 thoughts every day. That's a staggering 4,375 thoughts for each and every one of your waking hours, or 72 thoughts per minute!

There is a constant stream of thoughts running through your mind and they tend to reflect the overall tone of your beliefs about yourself. Whatever you see in yourself, you see mirrored in your world. You can't change all of your thoughts, but you can change the overall tone of your thinking.

I mentioned the importance of affirming to yourself and others that you are already a happy person. "I am happy" is an example of the type of affirmative statements you want to begin to make about yourself both in your head and aloud, and to repeat as often as possible.

Your core beliefs are like solid rock. However, water can dissolve rock over time, and each time you make a positive statement about yourself you drip water onto the rock of belief. In time the rock will erode. You will begin to feel lovable and worthy and, most of all, happy!

There are four attributes to the types of statements you want to make, and each begins with the letter P. Your statements should be:

1. Personal
2. Present
3. Positive
4. Powerful

Personal

Speak in the first person. Always use the word "I." In Chapter 3, I explained how to separate from the ego, giving it its own voice. When the ego speaks, it should be articulated in the second person addressing you as "you." However, we are now speaking as our genuine self and so you should use the word "I."

Present

Affirm that you are what you say you are here and now. Ali didn't say, "I'll defeat Frazier and Foreman and others and then I *will be* the greatest. He said, "I *am* the greatest! "Here, now, current, present tense. As we mentioned, in the realm of spirit, there is no past or future, there is only now. In these statements you are bolstering your spirit and stating boldly that the attributes you ascribe to yourself are already present.

Powerful

Commanding words engage your enthusiasm and focus your mind. If something is exciting and compelling, it tends to get your attention and to drive the idea more deeply into your subconscious.

Positive

Your words must be upbeat. They must affirm an optimal level of existence. The more positive your words are, the more they dilute the negative words that tend to run unchecked in your mind.

Here are some examples:

- I am very happy.
  - **I** (personal) **am** (present) **very** (powerful) **happy** (positive).
- I am dearly loved.

- ° **I** (personal) **am** (present) **dearly** (powerful) **loved** (positive).

- I am certain that this experience is leading to something good.

  - ° **I** (personal) **am** (present) **certain** (powerful) **that this is experience is leading to something good** (positive).

Designate certain times for saying your positive statements aloud. Develop your own schedule for making this ritual habitual. You might do this while brushing your teeth. As you gaze into the bathroom mirror, continue to brush until you have made 10 positive statements about yourself. Do this every morning and every evening.

Personally, I do this while I'm shaving in the shower. Because I not only shave my face but my head as well, I have five to seven minutes to repeat hundreds of laudatory things about myself.

Anything that makes you appreciate yourself more fully increases the feeling that you are worthy of being happy.

Here are some more examples:

- *The universe is conspiring for my good.*
- *God loves me and wants me to be happy.*
- *I love my life!*
- *Something great is going to happen to me today.*
- *I have valuable gifts and talents to share, and the world compensates me well for what I offer!*
- *I am really attractive!*
- *I am smart!*

To think well of yourself does not diminish others. Your comments are not comparing you to anyone, rather they are affirming your belief in your innate goodness and value. The more often you make such statements, the more you shift the overall tone of your thoughts. Whenever you think about it, say something nice to yourself, because chances are you have decades of making negative statements to yourself to overcome.

I know a man named Morgan who speaks harshly about himself whenever he makes even the slightest mistake. One day I was seated next to Morgan at conference table and as he reached for a legal pad, he accidentally knocked his pen to the floor. As he leaned over to retrieve his pen, he muttered, "Way to go, dummy!" I have heard Morgan refer to himself as an idiot, a jerk, a loser, and many other destructive things.

Of course, this is Morgan's ego speaking, not him, but it has become habitual for him to let his ego criticize him at every turn. This man is *not* a happy person.

Today you will have 70,000 thoughts bouncing around in your mind and many of them will be fearful, judgmental, and self-critical. Speaking positive things about yourself dilutes this negativity and shifts your core belief about yourself. As your core belief changes, your conviction that you deserve to be happy becomes magnified.

Taking God's Name in Vain

There is a common misunderstanding regarding the third of what Christians and Hebrews call the Ten Commandments. The commandment is, "You shall not take the name of the Lord your God in vain."

When something is "in vain" it means that it is without value. To take the name of God in vain means to use God's name as if it were meaningless.

What, then, is the name of God?

In Exodus 3:13 we read, "And Moses said unto God, Behold, when I come unto the children of Israel, and shall say unto them, The God of your fathers has sent me unto you; and they shall say to me, What is his name? What shall I say unto them?"

According to this Old Testament story, God answers Moses saying that his name is, "I AM."

Whenever you say "I am" followed by a negative statement about yourself, you are taking the Lord's name in vain.

To say "I am" and then follow it with a positive statement is a testament to your own innate value as an expression of the divine. This is not arrogant; this is true humility, as it declares that you are one with Spirit and not separate.

Develop a time to speak positively to and about yourself and repeat the process as often as you can. The great speaker and author Denis Waitley offers some sound advice: "When you're talking to yourself, watch your language."

THE OTHER MAGIC WORDS

A few years ago, I took a class given by a great spiritual teacher who gave us what proved to be a difficult assignment. "Whenever someone pays you a compliment," she said, "don't lessen the praise. Instead, simply respond by saying 'Thank you, this is true, I accept.'"

A compliment is a gift. To discount the compliment or dispute its validity is not only rude, but it diminishes the value of the gift.

Earlier this week I attended a yoga class given by a woman who was filling in for the regular instructor. I knew that this was one of the first classes this woman had taught, and when it was over I went up to her and said, "That was a great class!"

She looked sheepish and said, "Oh, I don't know. I guess it was all right. I made some mistakes. I really just wanted to try in my own limited way to do okay so that the regular teacher wouldn't be too disappointed."

As she spoke, I could feel my energy and the enthusiasm for everything we had accomplished seep away like air from a balloon.

Knowing this woman well and considering her a friend, I smiled and said, "What you mean to say is 'Thank you,' right?"

She pondered this for a moment and then said, "Well, yes, I guess so. I just want to feel worthy of your compliment."

"If you accept compliments when they come your way," I said, "you will begin to feel worthy of them."

A few days later I took her class again and at the end I told her how much I enjoyed myself. This time, she smiled broadly and said simply, "Thank you." We both laughed at this and I could tell she felt better for accepting my genuine compliment and allowing herself to feel deserving of it.

When someone gives you the gift of a compliment, do your best to say "Thank you, this is true, I accept." At a bare minimum, say "Thank you."

To cite another quote attributed to Gandhi, "Happiness is when what you think, what you say, and what you do are in harmony." In the next chapter we will explore how we take our happy thoughts and words and harmonize them into actions.

RECAPPING "WORDS OF HAPPINESS"

- Your thoughts come from your words but your words impact your thoughts.

- Remember the magic word "Abracadabra"—"I have created through my speech!"

- Pray affirmatively using the acronym ACT: **A**cknowledge the Presence of the Divine, **C**laim a Positive Outcome, and Give **T**hanks.

- Speak positive statements to yourself that are **P**ersonal, **P**resent, **P**ositive, and **P**owerful.

- When people pay you a compliment, accept their gift by saying thank you.

CHAPTER FIVE

Actions of Happiness

However many holy words you read,
However many you speak,
What good will they do you
If you do not act on upon them?
—The Buddha

W hen you feel happy, you tend to smile.

When you smile, you tend to feel happy.

Several studies have found that the simple action of smiling fires off happiness receptors within our brains. One study found that people who suffered from facial paralysis tended to be less happy overall, not because of their physical malady but because they could no longer frame their faces into smiles.

EXPERIMENTING WITH SMILES

A study conducted in 1988 by social psychologist Fritz Strack manipulated participants' facial expressions to test whether forming a smile can improve a person's mood. Participants were told that the study was actually to uncover how people who had lost the ability to use their hands adapted to everyday activities such as writing and operating a television remote. Each participant was given a pencil to be held in his or her mouth and was asked to complete a series of tasks using the pencil.

Several subjects were required to hold the pencil between their teeth causing them to pull back their lips forming a smile. Others were instructed to hold the pencil between their lips, which prevented them from smiling.

After attempting the activities holding the pencils in either their teeth or their mouths, subjects in both groups were then asked to rate the humor level of several cartoons. The subjects holding the pencils in their teeth, who had been forced to smile, found the same cartoons significantly funnier than the other group. A smile—even when forced—made the cartoons more enjoyable.

Without a doubt, the action of smiling can make you feel happier. Because of the interconnectedness of your mind and body, it can be difficult to get yourself to smile when you are not feeling happy, but if you can force yourself to hold a smile for several minutes, you will soon find your happiness level increasing.

Not only will smiling cause you to feel happier in the short-term, a smile sets an intention for happiness in your future. In a 2001 study, researchers interviewed a group of women as to how happy they considered themselves to be. They then went back and looked at these women's college yearbook photos from 1958 and 1960 and found that the women who smiled the broadest in their college annuals reported being the happiest women in the study more than four decades later.

A Picture Is Worth a Thousand Smiles

A 2012 study, published in *Social Psychological and Personality Science*, found that college students who posted Facebook profile pictures showing themselves smiling broadly reported being happier three years later that those who had posted photos with less intense smiles.

The coauthors of the paper detailing this study, J. Patrick Seder and Shigehiro Oishi, psychologists at the University of Virginia wrote, "The expression of positive affect captured in a photograph can convey surprisingly rich information about people's long-term well being."

There is an old saying "pictures don't lie." If a camera catches you with an immense and genuine smile, it is an indication that you are sending a ripple of happiness that is going to travel downstream into your future. Smiling is one of the simplest and most important actions you can take to become a happier person.

Your actions are one of the key ingredients to being a happy person. Nineteenth-century British prime minister Benjamin Disraeli observed, "Action may not always bring happiness, but there is no happiness without action."

The Formula for Happiness

Four prominent psychologists (Sonja Lyubomirsky, Ken Sheldon, David Schkade, and Martin Seligman) have found a formula for happiness, and actions (or, as they call them, "voluntary activities") are a key ingredient.

The formula for happiness is:

$$H = S + C + V$$

H = *Happiness* S = *Set Point*

C = *Conditions of Life* V = *Voluntary Activities*

Happiness is a combination of your **S**et Point, **C**onditions of Life, and **V**oluntary Activities, or actions.

As we have discussed, when you set a happiness set point goal using a scale from 1 (very unhappy) to 10 (ecstatically happy) and monitor how happy you are relative to your goal, you can increase and maintain a higher level of happiness.

Conditions of Life, the second factor, tend to be the happiness ingredient most people think has the greatest impact on their level of happiness. If the conditions of life are going well, a person is happy, right?

Well, no, not really. An article published in the *Proceedings of the National Academy of Sciences* reports that conditions of life account for only about 10% your overall happiness.

It seems counterintuitive but the conditions of your life have only a minimal impact on your overall happiness.

Take that in for a minute. The conditions of our lives—which include but are not limited to our health, our relationships, our income, the economy, our job, the weather, our children treating us with respect, whether we find a good parking space at the mall, getting a good night's sleep, and much more—account for only 10% of our overall level of happiness.

Grasping this concept can be very liberating. If you remind yourself that regardless of what transpires during the day, 90% of your happiness will be unaffected, it can substantially lessen worry, fear, and anxiety. This release from being concerned about what may or may not happen frees you to feel content, and contentment equals happiness.

Unfortunately, most people dwell in the shadows and fear life's conditions. They ruminate, "If only my job were better," "If only I lost twenty pounds," "If only there were a Republican president," "If only I earned another fifty thousand dollars a year," "If only she would call," "If only my back would stop hurting," etc.

If a magic genie showed up and gave you *everything* you think you want, the net effect after your initial glee would only be a possible increase of somewhere around 10%.

According to the article in the *Proceedings of the National Academy of Sciences*, 50% of happiness is determined by the happiness set point. Life conditions account for only 10% and actions account for 40%—that's nearly half of your overall level of happiness.

Several actions have been identified that can make you feel happier:

- Smiling
- Doing something nice for someone else
- Exercising regularly
- Getting enough sleep
- Eating with proper nutrition
- Engaging in meaningful and fulfilling work
- Having a close-knit community
- Freeing your life of clutter
- Releasing resentments
- Cultivating and expressing gratitude
- Feeling a spiritual connection and a having a spiritual practice

We already talked about the importance of smiling and the importance of meaningful and engaging work. Having a lot of clutter in your life can make you feel overwhelmed and distracted. Taking a day or so to put things in order and then putting things back every time you use them lowers your stress level and increases your sense of well-being.

Take a look at this list and see how many of these actions are a part of your life. Take one item at a time and commit to working on it for a few weeks until it becomes habitual and then move on to the next.

Your level of happiness can be likened to a deep snowfall. Each individual positive action you take adds to your level of happiness just as each tiny snowflake adds to the depth and coverage of the snow.

In this chapter, I'm going to share with you a handful of actions that are more like buckets of snow than individual flakes. Making these actions part of your life will immediately and significantly increase your level of happiness.

IT HAPPENS IN THE KITCHEN

Several years ago, I was in the locker room of my local gym. I saw a man there who I had seen quite often. During the previous year, he and I had exchanged pleasant greetings whenever we passed each other but we never spoke at length.

The reason we did not talk more in depth is that it was obvious from his thick accent that he barely spoke English. He had mastered, "Hello," "It is nice to see you"—always overemphasizing each syllable, and "Good-bye." Beyond that, he seemed incapable of communicating with me and the other men in the locker room.

When I first met this man, he was not in very good shape. He was of average height with very little muscle mass and he was about 35 pounds overweight. I would often see him in the gym working hard lifting weights and doing cardio, but his efforts seemed to have little effect on his physique.

I injured my back playing racquetball and was out for a few months. On the day of my return, I was changing clothes in the locker room when a very fit man said hello from over my shoulder. I recognized the clipped cadence of the man and turned around with a smile. My smile faded into disbelief as I saw the man I had greeted so many times. In the 90 or so days that I had been gone, he had completely transformed his body.

He could see the shock on my face, and with a smile, he said in broken English, "It happened in the kitchen, not just in the gym."

His comment has stuck with me. This man's metamorphosis was as much the result of his nutrition as his exercise regimen.

Mental Nutrition

Physical fitness is a result of exercise—what you do with your body, and nutrition—what you put into your body. Happiness is also the result of exercise—what you do with your mind, and nutrition—what you put into your mind.

Up until now we have talked a lot about mental exercises that lead to higher levels of happiness. We've talked about the importance of harnessing your thoughts and dismissing your ego's input, and we have examined how your words reflect and impact your thinking. Now, let's talk about nutrition. But, before we go into the kitchen, let's consider *drugs* and nutrition.

- The best-selling prescription drug in the United Sates is Lipitor, an anticholesterol drug, with annual sales exceeding $7.7 billion.

- The third-best-selling drug in the United States is the antacid Nexium, with $6.2 billion in sales.

- Crestor, another anticholesterol drug, is the eighth-best-selling drug in the America, with revenues of $4.4 billion.

These are only the best-selling prescription anticholesterol and antacid drugs; there are many more. In addition, Americans also spend in excess of $10 billion every year on over-the-counter antacids.

Between prescription and over-the-counter drugs, Americans spend in the neighborhood of $40 *billion* every single year on drugs to counteract their poor nutrition choices.

If your dog suffered from chronic upset stomach and/or high cholesterol, chances are that the first thing you would do is change his diet. However, when it comes to ourselves we either fail to see the connection between what we eat and our health or we consider it too much of hardship to make healthier choices, and so we take pills with potentially harmful side effects rather than improve our nutrition.

If you change what goes into your body, you will change what goes on with your body.

When it comes to mental nutrition, Americans seem similarly inclined to mask the result of their poor choices rather than make new choices.

- In the last two decades, antidepressant use in the United States has jumped a staggering 400%. Today, at least 1 in 10 people take prescription medication to elevate their mood, and antidepressant medications are the second-most-profitable classification of prescription drugs.

- In addition to prescription drugs, 1 in 15 Americans abuse illegal drugs.

- A study by the US Department of Justice found that nearly 1 in 4 Americans consume alcohol at "hazardous" levels.

Of course, there is certainly some overlap in these statistics, but conservatively this means that somewhere between 20% and 50% of Americans regularly take substances as artificial replacements for happiness or to numb the pain of their unhappiness.

Change What Goes *Into* Your Mind and You Will Change What Goes *On In* Your Mind

If you made a resolution to become fitter, part of your program would be to change your nutrition.

You have made a resolution to become *happy this year*, and to make your resolution a reality requires that you change your mental nutrition.

Thomas Cardinal Wolsey is said to have warned, "Be very, very careful what you put into that head, because you will never, ever get it out." Begin now to replace your poor mental nutrition choices with healthy ones.

A Happiness Mental Diet Program

Stop watching, reading, and listening to the "news."
I always put "news" in quotations when referring to what is delivered to us as news programming because it is in many ways just fearmongering. What is commonly called "news" is actually an attempt to frighten and upset you so that you will continue to consume what is being shoveled. Don't let "news" be a part of your mental diet. Especially, don't consume "news" right before bedtime, because this negativity will fester in your subconscious while you sleep.

Start seeking out inspirational stories and reading inspirational literature.
There are myriad resources dedicated to personal growth and the triumph of the human spirit. Here are a handful of suggestions to be found on the web:

- HappyThisYear.com
- ToYouLoveGod.org
- AComplaintFreeWorld.org
- Entheos.com/PhilosophersNotes
- GratitudeHabitat.com
- LifeToFullest.com
- EnjoySpirituality.org
- SelfHelpDaily.com
- Inspire21.com

Personally, I always have an inspirational audiobook playing on my smartphone when I'm dressing, driving, or doing chores around the house.

Stop associating with people who are predominantly in their "pain-body."

In *A New Earth*, Eckhart Tolle explains that everyone has what he calls a "pain-body"—a part of us that actually enjoys living in pain, angst, and drama. As human beings, we know that we are alive only through stimulation and sensations. Unfortunately, most people are habituated to experiencing life through negative stimulation and painful sensations.

Such people complain constantly about other people and situations. They find fault with anything and everything. They are often not aware of their penchant for negativity but they live in a self-created and self-perpetuating toxic environment of blame, shame, guilt, anger, and resentment.

If you are around these types of people, you consume their negativity and it becomes a part of who you are. Even if these people are part of your family, avoid them as much as you can.

Start seeking out the happiest and most upbeat people you can find, and spend as much time with them as possible.

Human beings tend to mirror those they are with, and as you associate with upbeat and happy people, you will begin to rise to their level of happiness.

Who is the happiest person you know? Invite that person to lunch or to have coffee. Listen to how he or she speaks, and attempt to talk the same way.

If you are fortunate, this person may hook you up with his or her friends and, because like attracts like, they will probably be happy as well. You will greatly expand your circle of happy associates.

Stop listening to heartache and breakup songs.

Two years ago, a friend of mine recommended that I try this, and I was amazed at the impact it had on my level of happiness. I used to enjoy listening to songs about lost love and the struggles of life, because I felt them stir me emotionally. What I discovered is that the stirring I felt was actually low-grade emotional pain.

With some songs that I liked because I thought they made me feel nostalgic, I realized that I was confusing nostalgia with melancholy.

Don't listen to songs about unfaithful relationships or violence, either. Both of these types of songs cultivate negative emotions that dilute your happiness.

Start noticing songs that celebrate life rather than condemn it.

Look for songs that make you feel inspired and that have a positive message. Create playlists on your smartphone or MP3 player, or make CDs, and put yourself on a strict diet of only songs that make you feel happy.

I have created several playlists for my iPhone that include such songs. Some are songs from nearly a half century ago and others are current. Here are some of my favorite happiness-inducing songs:

- "Here Comes the Sun" – I like the version by Richie Havens

- "Be the Change" – MC Yogi
- "Oh, What a Beautiful Morning" – Ray Charles
- "Internal Heights" – Trevor Hall
- "Bright Side of the Road" – Van Morrison
- "We Let it Be" – Rickie Byars Beckwith
- "Safe, Secure, Peaceful, Satisfied" – Bukeka Shoals
- "Get Together" – The Youngbloods
- "Born Free" – Kid Rock
- "Don't Stop" – Fleetwood Mac
- "Firework" – Katy Perry
- "Hope" – Shaggy
- "I Feel Fine" – The Beatles
- "Take It Any Way You Want It" – The Outlaws
- "Hold On Tight" – ELO
- "Imagine the Impossible" – Zapped
- "Roll with It" – Steve Winwood
- "Walking on Sunshine" – Katrina & The Waves
- "Hold On" – Wilson Phillips
- "Accentuate the Positive" – The Sunnysiders
- "I Just Want to Celebrate" – Rare Earth

Several studies have found that listening to music with pro-social and positive lyrics leads to a statistically significant increase in positive mood, whereas listening to antisocial and downbeat lyrics lead to a negative impact on a person's mood state. An article by life coach Joe Wilner on PsychCentral.com states, "If you're looking for a boost of energy or a pick me up, music may be just what you need. When we listen to upbeat, rhythmic music it can arouse and inspire us to be more productive and enthusiastic. Music can be revitalizing and get us to take action, keep us alert, and maintain a cheerful attitude."

You can use the power of music to either increase or decrease your level of happiness, depending upon the lyrics and energy of the songs you select.

If you doubt that the content of the songs you hear can impact your mental and emotional state, consider this: While I was writing this, I heard an interview on National Public Radio with a former neo-Nazi skinhead. This man shared that it was once his job to recruit teenage boys who would adopt this organization's violent and racist philosophies and join.

"How did you get seemingly normal, healthy teens to join a group dedicated to hate, violence, and prejudice?" the interviewer asked.

"It was so easy," said the former skinhead. "I would ride around with young guys my age and would tell them the music they were listening to was crap. I'd then throw their tapes out the car window—this was during the days of cassettes; and I'd say, 'Dig on this' as I slipped in a mix tape of songs that were violent and racist."

"I knew that if I could get them to listen to one of these tapes over and over," he continued, "they would ultimately join us. Music is that powerful."

Some songs are nutritious, while others are like candy. Some songs are like junk food and others are downright poisonous.

If a song with a painful or negative message comes on the radio and you don't have a positive playlist ready, switch off the radio and practice your ACT method of praying, practice your "I am" statements, or even sing a happy song to yourself. Or put a big smile on your face and see how long you can keep it there.

Stop watching violent movies and television shows. And stop reading books about such topics. Also cut out the violent video games.

Again, I thought this was a little drastic until I began to try it. When you take in violent images and themes, you begin to respond energetically to them and they resound throughout your mind.

Dozens of studies have found that consuming violent media content leads to people feeling and acting more aggressively. Now, a study by the Education Resources Information Center finds that the more violent programming children watch, *the more they tend to see the world as frightening, hostile, and less friendly.* These sensations stand in opposition to a happy mind-set.

Regardless of our age, taking in violent programming has an effect on our sense of well-being, which is, by definition, how happy we are.

Eckhart Tolle says that most movies are "made for pain-bodies by pain-bodies." Most people are not happy because they are trapped in their pain-body, and the movies, TV shows, and games they watch reinforce this state. You can't be happy when you are saturated in pain. Giving up books, movies, and television shows about painful subjects deactivates your pain-body, allowing you to feel happier.

Please understand that this not a moral condemnation of this type of media. I'm not saying you "should" give up violent content because it is "wrong." I'm saying that when you cease to allow violence into your mind, you will experience greater peace and happiness.

When I was a boy, I would take the bus from our home to downtown to attend the all-day Saturday *Monster Movie*

Marathons at the Ritz Theater. For 75¢, I could while away an afternoon sitting in the dark, being scared by Frankenstein, Dracula, The Wolfman, The Thing, The Blob, and an endless array of flesh-eating zombies.

As I grew older, my passion for these movies continued even while the genre was becoming more gory and explicit. Horror was no longer enough to tantalize me. I now watched an endless stream of slasher films like *A Nightmare on Elm Street*, *Halloween*, and *Friday the 13th*. Even as an adult, I never missed a movie designed to scare me. As movies such as *Saw*, *Hostel*, and *Scream* pushed the limits of gore and violence, I watched them all.

It has now been several years since I've watched a horror movie and I've discovered a couple of very interesting things:

1. These movies are addictive. Watching a scary movie causes us to feel terror, which causes our bodies to release endorphins, giving us a mild feeling of euphoria.
2. Even though these movies make us feel high, they come with a hefty price tag. They ramp up our pain-bodies into overdrive, and we vibrate at a level of fear and anxiety that endures for hours or even days. They also make us more fearful about life, which leads to unhappiness.
3. These movies can have a direct negative effect on happiness.

Now answer these questions:

*   *Have you ever awakened from a pleasant dream feeling happy?*
*   *Have you ever awakened from an upsetting dream feeling unhappy?*

- *Have you noticed that if you wake up in a happy mood, it is easier to maintain that mood throughout the day?*

- *Have you noticed that if you wake up in a bad mood, it can be hard to shake?*

For most of my life, I regularly had unhappy and frightening dreams. In retrospect, given the steady diet of death and dismemberment I was feeding my mind, this is not surprising. Many mornings I awoke with a nightmare hangover that made me feel unhappy for hours. I projected out unhappiness, the world reflected it back to me, and it created a loop that played out over and over. At that time I never saw the connection between gory movies, nightmares, and unhappiness.

However, since I stopped watching violent movies and horror films, I rarely, if ever, have a bad dream. As a result, I tend to wake up at a higher level of happiness, making it easier to maintain and increase my happiness for the rest of the day.

Don't fill your mental Crock-Pot with terrorizing and violent images. They will stew in your subconscious while you sleep and you'll get to eat them for breakfast!

Consider that you, like most people, have an addiction to violence because it actually gives you an endorphin kick. Begin to wean yourself away from such poisonous entertainment and discover for yourself how much better you feel.

Start watching movies and television shows that make you feel happy.

When you are making your choice as to what films and televisions shows will get a slice of your precious leisure time, be as selective about the content as you would be about which contain your favorite actors.

At first, you will be surprised by how much modern entertainment is centered on violent, negative, and painful things. Soon, however, you'll begin to find movies and shows that make you feel good about people and your world.

Here are two additional feel-good suggestions:

- Get a free trial membership to Spiritual Cinema Circle (SpiritualCinemaCircle.com).

- Search YouTube for words such as "inspiration," "funny," "inspiring," "positive," "motivational," "upbeat," and other keywords.

I've had YouTube parties where friends will come over with their best suggestions for things they find funny or inspiring and we'll spend the evening sharing and enjoying each other's suggestions.

Select programs that make you laugh and depict characters with positive qualities you would like to emulate.

And if you have a guilty pleasure, don't worry about it. An occasional splurge is not going to completely wreck your diet; nor will an occasionally violent show permanently lower your level of happiness. Chances are, however, you will not find them as satisfying and may actually feel uncomfortable as you become aware of your mind and even your body reacting to the violence.

As previously mentioned, I existed on a diet of entertainment junk food until just a few years ago. Last week, I went to see a movie that was highly rated. I knew that it had some violence, though it wasn't the overall tone of the movie. I was enjoying the story, but about halfway through there was an extended scene where the hero and the villain slugged it out for a full five minutes. The thuds echoing through the theater's subwoofers and the sounds of bones breaking made me feel very anxious. It was as if someone were hitting me!

I left the theater and told the management I'd like to see something funny instead and they graciously let me see another movie.

I'm not complaining then or now. I don't begrudge anyone watching violence; I've just gotten to where my level of happiness is too important, and violence sends a negative effect that ripples for hours through my psyche.

Myriad studies show that consuming violent content desensitizes people to violence—especially children. Research shows that if a person watches violent television and movies, he or she begins to take in violence as an acceptable norm. Consuming violence attunes one to violence and can make that person more likely to act aggressively—not exactly behavior that is conducive to happiness!

If You're Not Ready to Dive In, At Least Wade
Whew! This mental nutrition list of **START**s and **STOP**s may seem a little daunting.

If it seems overwhelming, consider taking just a 10-day fast from negativity and violence. Mark your calendar and for the next 10 days, stop watching the "news," avoid negative people and sad songs, and eliminate your exposure to violence. Instead, watch and read inspirational and uplifting media, hang around with happy people, and listen to upbeat music.

Then honestly evaluate how you feel.

If you feel happier, try it for another 10 days or so. Take it easy with yourself. There's no rush. If jumping in for 10 days seems too daunting, pick just one of these suggestions and do it for 10 days. Then try another and another.

Or pick one day of the week and make it a "mental health day" each week, in which you only consume songs and entertainment that are positive and upbeat.

If you're wondering if this is necessary, go back to the description you wrote out as to how your life will be when you are a happy person (the exercise we did in Chapter 2) and ask yourself how negative people, painful songs, and violent content fit in with the ideal happy self you have created. Chances are you'll see that to be the happy person you have resolved to become this year, you're going to leave some things behind.

Three years ago, I read a couple of books on the health benefits of becoming vegan—not eating meat of any kind as well eliminating all animal products, such as eggs and cheese from one's diet. When I read these books, here is what I remember thinking:

1. "If I gave up meat, eggs, and dairy, what would I eat? Would my diet consist of nothing but salads and sprouts? I don't want to live my life eating bland foods."
2. "I don't think I can give up meat, eggs, and dairy. I enjoy eating them."

Finally, I decided to give it a try for just one day.

Eating vegan was odd because it was unfamiliar, but I soon found that there are a *lot* of delicious things to eat other than animal products. I've now been eating vegan for two years and I've lost an additional 10 pounds. My doctor recently did a workup of my blood and found that, among other good news, my "bad" cholesterol level is less than half what is considered acceptable and my testosterone level is at the high end of normal. Further, a scan of my heart's arteries found zero plaque, meaning that I have virtually no chance of having a heart attack.

In short, I thought that I could never change my nutrition because I thought I would be giving up too much. In reality, it was not difficult at all and I'm much healthier for the change. More important, I have discovered all types of delicious meals and restaurants.

I was recently speaking to someone at a conference dinner and he noticed I was eating grilled vegetables, sautéed tofu, and wild rice while everyone else was eating medium rare steak. When I told him I was vegan, he said, "When you became vegan, didn't you have to give up a lot?"

No one had ever asked me that question before. I thought a minute and responded, "Yes. I did have to give up a lot."

He smiled sympathetically, but I surprised both him and myself as I continued, "I had to give up ten pounds of body fat. I gave up acid reflux, high cholesterol, bad morning breath, after-meal sluggishness, feeling bloated and tired, irritability, high blood pressure, constipation. . ." My list continued and I realized for the first time that better physical nutrition might seem like a process of "giving up" but, in reality, it is a process of "gaining." The same is true for mental nutrition.

Remember the words of the man from the locker room, "It happened in the kitchen, not just in the gym." Begin to carefully select what goes into your mind, knowing that the nourishment choices you make will significantly impact how happy you are.

WHAT'S GOOD ABOUT IT?

One morning I woke up feeling stressed and overwhelmed. I had so many challenges, deadlines, tasks, and difficulties. The weight of it all felt like an anvil crushing my chest.

After several minutes of feeling miserable, I rolled out of bed, picked up my journal, grabbed a cup of coffee, and headed for my deck.

I sat down and began to make a list of the myriad difficulties I was facing. I gave myself permission to write down on paper *all* of my challenges, fears, concerns, slights—every single thing that was causing me worry and consternation.

I wrote until I had completely purged my mind of everything that had been upsetting me. I glanced down and read the list. It consisted of only nine things.

"That's it?" I said aloud. "All that fear and stress over just nine things?" Prior to journaling, I had felt hopelessly overburdened and yet I realized that even less than 10 issues had felt like an overwhelming burden.

Why? Because my focus was on those nine things.

I then began to make a list of everything that was going well in my life. I wrote down every blessing I was experiencing. The list went on for nearly 10 pages, and after an hour and a half of writing out all the good things in my life, I realized that I had significantly more to be grateful for than I had challenges.

I looked back at my list of nine challenges and realized that six of them were beyond my control. I couldn't do anything about them. I decided to let them go, do what I could on the other three, and keep my focus on my list of positive things. My mood took a dramatic upward turn and stayed there.

The Expressway to Happiness

In all of my research on happiness, I have found that the one thing all experts agree upon is that making a list of things for which you are grateful is the best on-ramp to the expressway to happiness.

Inspirational speaker Esther Hicks calls this a "Rampage of Appreciation." Making a list, stating aloud or recounting in your mind all of the things you have to be grateful for will bump your happiness level up quickly, and continuing to remind yourself of all the blessings in your life will keep it there.

I have a friend who is a type 2 diabetic. Several times each day he measures his blood sugar to make certain it is within a healthy range. For your overall happiness to increase, it is important to watch your happiness level with the same diligence as my friend checks his blood sugar level. To be free from unhappiness is to be diligent in maintaining a high level of happiness.

What do you do if you find your happiness level dipping? Immediately begin to make note of everything in your life for which you are thankful.

Everything!

For example, from where I sit right now, I can observe many things I am grateful for, including my computer, my mouse, my keyboard, my large monitor, my great speakers, the sound of the wind gently blowing outside, the cool afternoon in the middle of what has been a very hot summer, the dove that has laid eggs in one of my hanging baskets, the tea I am sipping, my glasses that allow me to read, and the windows that allow me enjoy the outside without having bugs enter my office.

Typing that list of things that I am thankful for just now took me less than 30 seconds and I could have gone on for another 10 minutes without even turning my head. If I had, I could have typed for another 20 to 30 minutes, listing only items in my office for which I am grateful.

As a result of this activity, I am happier now than I was a mere two minutes ago.

Becoming 25% Happier

In his book *Thanks!: How Practicing Gratitude Can Make You Happier*, Robert Emmons of the University of California, Davis, cites research he conducted into the powerful effects of gratitude on happiness.

Emmons brought together three groups of students and had them keep a daily journal noting their moods, physical health, and general attitudes, to be used as benchmarks for comparison at the end the experiment.

The study, which lasted 10 weeks, required one of the groups of students to write down five things they were grateful for each day.

A second group was asked to make a daily list of five things they considered to be some of the hassles of everyday living, such as taxes and trying to find a parking space.

The third group was asked to write down five events that happened during the previous week, without instruction that the events be considered positive or negative.

At the end of the study, members of the first group—the group that wrote down five things each day for which they were grateful, reported being a full *25% happier* than the people in the other two groups!

Simply writing down five things each day for which they were grateful increased the subjective well-being (happiness) of these students by a quarter. That's truly significant.

How would you like to be 25% happier than you are now? It's as easy as taking a couple of minutes every day to write down five things that you are thankful for.

In the previous chapter we discussed the happiness-inducing power of speaking affirmatively—making statements that are **P**ersonal, **P**resent, **P**ositive, and **P**owerful. Stating "I am grateful for [this or that]" combines your positive statement with the power of gratitude.

You may discover that when your happiness level begins to turn south, once you start your "Rampage of Appreciation" there is typically a lag of about a minute or so before you start to feel happier. This is because you have to turn the tide of unhappiness, but once the happy feelings began to flow, they will continue.

In Everything, Give Thanks

1 Thessalonians 5:18 in the Christian Bible reads, "In everything give thanks." Note that the apostle Paul isn't saying "*for* everything give thanks." Giving thanks for flat tires, coffee spilled on your new pants, lost car keys, and toothaches is not practical. However, if you follow Paul's advice and "*in* everything give thanks," you can keep your happiness at the highest possible level even during the day-to-day difficulties of life.

Gratitude should not be just an automatic response to getting something you want. It should be an ongoing expression of appreciation for having what you've got. There are hundreds of things within an arm's reach of you right now that, if they were gone, you would miss. Each of these things is suitable material for you to focus your gratitude upon.

In many ways, being a happier person is about dismissing unhappiness. It's as if there were two forces shifting back and forth in your head, attempting to seize predominance. Repeating "thank you, thank you, thank you," and being specific about all that you have to be grateful for, negates the negativity that assaults you on a daily basis from other people and the "news." Thirteenth-century German philosopher Meister Eckhart is believed to have said, "If the only prayer you ever said in your whole life was 'Thank you,' that would suffice."

By now, you may be thinking, "Isn't this just a bunch of positive thinking stuff?"

Again, I say yes. In his decades of research into positive psychology, Martin Seligman has found that happiness is inseparable from a positive frame of mind. A positive mind is one that sees a large number of things to appreciate. A negative mind sees a large number of things with which to find fault.

Happiness comes from shifting our minds, and the fastest way to do this is to make a gratitude list.

FOCUS ON THE BOX

Why do jigsaw puzzle manufacturers print a picture of the completed puzzle on the top of the box? The answer is, of course, so you can know what the finished puzzle will look like and this knowledge will guide you on where to place the pieces.

Read and reread your answers to the questions in Chapter 2. Develop a clear understanding of how your life will be different when you are happier. As you do, your new, happier self will emerge. Having this vivid image of how your life will be when you are happier is like looking at the picture on top of a puzzle box so you know where to put all the pieces of your life.

If your overall aim is to be happy—that is to say, if you want to measure your life based on how happy you are—where, for example, does the puzzle piece of family fit in? How about your job piece? Where does your health piece fit? And what about your spirituality piece? As you gaze at the image of yourself being a happy person, where do you fit leisure time?

Keeping a clear focus on how your life will be when you are significantly and sustainably happier keeps you on track. Remember: Everything you *think* you want is actually something you believe will make you feel happier. Knowing how your life will be when you are happier helps you see everything else as a means to your ultimate end of happiness, rather than the other way around.

For myself, I wrote out my vision of my "happy life" a year ago on a giant three-foot-by-two-foot piece of paper and pinned it to the wall next to my bed, so that it is the first thing I see every morning.

I roll out of bed and remind myself that nothing I do that day is more important than being happy. *Rather than happiness being the result of my activities, happiness should be the cause of them.* My goal is to do and accomplish whatever brings me happiness.

Making happiness your highest priority as the key determinant of your activities puts a whole new spin on life. This should be your first and predominant goal. Then decide what you want to do with your life.

Some people get confused and afraid when they hear this suggestion. They become concerned that such an approach would lead to anarchy and chaos. Further, many believe that putting your own happiness first is being selfish.

In reality, if more people were to put their happiness first, it would make the world a much better place, because you can't raise your own happiness level without impacting those around you.

Wouldn't you like to be with a happier spouse, happier children, happier employees, happier store clerks, happier government employees, and happier friends? If these people put their own happiness as their highest priority, we would benefit from their more positive state.

It is simply more agreeable to be around a happy person. Happiness is like rain to a parched and barren land. Our happiness is a gift we bestow upon others.

The Ripple Effect

A few months ago, a woman named Pat Schatswell moved into the home across from mine. As soon as she moved in, our neighborhood began to improve.

Pat placed several beautiful flowering plants in front of her home. As I sat outside enjoying my morning coffee, I savored the spectacle of her flowers and watched the variety of birds that came to her feeders.

A few days later, I noticed that the neighbor to my right had also purchased flowering plants and placed them in front of her home. Soon, the neighbor across from her did likewise.

That weekend I found myself at a home improvement store and I decided to purchase a few outdoor flowering arrangements to place in front of my own home. The following day, I noticed another neighbor had purchased flowers for her yard, and then another and another. Flowers began to spring up all along both sides of the street until our neighborhood took on a glorious new look and feel.

And it all began because Pat had decided to place flowering plants in front of her home. The other day while she was out walking her aging schnauzer, Roxanne, I called to Pat and remarked how she had started a trend that had spread throughout the neighborhood. I asked her what had inspired her to put out the flowers.

She looked surprised and responded in her quiet mid-Missouri drawl, "I didn't put the flowers out to get other people to do anything." She then shrugged her shoulders and said, "I just like flowers."

Pat had put the flowers in front of her home because she liked flowers. She did it for herself. However, others responded to her actions and soon there were flowers everywhere—flowers that Pat now gets to enjoy.

When you set a resolution to increase your level of happiness, it may be because *you* want to enjoy an increased sense of well-being, but know that others around you will benefit as well. Not only that, there is a strong chance that they will begin to act happier around you and, just like Pat now gets to enjoy looking at her neighbors' flowers, you will get to enjoy their happiness radiated back to you. This will make you feel even happier, and you will radiate more happiness to others who will respond in kind. A happiness loop will be created that will feed on itself and magnify.

Keep your focus on the top of the puzzle box—your image of what you as a truly happy person is like.

Become a Happiness Junkie

Read everything you can about happiness. One study found that simply reading about happiness makes you happier. Just as a person who commits him or herself to becoming fit will begin to read books and magazines on diet and exercise, read whatever you can find on the subject of happiness.

As actor Harrison Ford put it, "Being happy is something you have to learn. I often surprise myself by saying 'Wow, this is it. I guess I'm happy. I got a home I love. A career that I love. I'm even feeling more and more at peace with myself.' If there's something else to happiness, let me know. I'm ambitious for that, too."

Be ambitious for happiness.

You have created the picture for the top of the box. Continue to study that picture and make certain that the puzzle pieces you put into place are going to make that picture a reality.

ORDER THE COMBO

I was on a speaking trip to Albuquerque, New Mexico, and, as is my custom, I went for a walk around the city as soon as I arrived.

The hotel where I was staying is across the street from a large city park, so I relaxed on a bench for an hour just taking in the energy of the city. A few hundred yards away, I could see an obviously impoverished woman try to stop everyone who came near her. I couldn't hear what she said, but it was obvious by her outstretched hand that she was asking for money.

Several well-dressed and seemingly affluent people walked quickly past her to avoid her gaze and her attempts to get their attention. This was not easy to do, as the woman was very persistent.

Again and again she approached strangers asking for help. Not a single one offered any assistance. They stared passed her and hurried along. I felt sad for her and started to walk over so that I could offer her some money.

As I drew nearer to her, I saw a young man on a bicycle approach the spot where the woman stood. The man had a scruffy beard and large-rimmed black glasses. He wore torn jeans and a faded gray T-shirt. I could see a bevy of tattoos on his arms and neck. Tied to the seat and dangling over the back wheel of the man's bike were two plastic bags overflowing with groceries.

I paused and watched as the harrowed woman stepped toward the young man, who leaned sharply to the left, swerving his bike to avoid her. The young man pedaled faster and rode away.

I turned my gaze to read a plaque on a statue and when I looked back, I saw the young man making a wide U-turn on his bike. He pulled up to where the old woman stood and stopped a few feet from her.

The two talked for a minute or two and then the young man reached into one of his grocery bags and pulled out a package of bagels. He handed them to the old woman, who clutched them to her chest. Even from the distance I could see a wide grin on her face.

The woman ripped open the bagels and began to munch greedily on one. The young man nodded his head and climbed back on his bike. He pedaled about 10 feet and then stopped. Looking over his shoulder, he began to speak to the woman again while still straddling the bike.

They talked as the woman gobbled down several of the cold, dry bagels. The man motioned ahead and the woman nodded. He dismounted the bike and began to push it slowly across the promenade. The old woman walked slowly alongside him.

As the two faded from my field of vision, I saw the man place a compassionate hand on the old woman's shoulder.

I stood for a long time replaying what had transpired. I remembered how I felt watching the many people who could have easily given this woman some money or bought her a meal, but who had chosen to walk past her as if she didn't exist.

I tried to put a name to what I felt watching how they had responded to her, and the word that seemed to fit was "unhappy." Although I had been a spectator and was not actually involved, seeing how they had dismissed her had left me with an empty, sad feeling.

I then thought about how I felt watching the young man's kindness and generosity. From the looks of their departure together, I presumed he was taking her to get a proper meal. Again, although I was a distant and silent witness to what transpired, watching his compassion and benevolence gave me a feeling I could only describe as "happy."

The Benevolent Desire of the Soul

How could the actions of people I had no formal connection with affect my level of happiness?

It will come as no surprise to you that the person who probably derived the most out this interaction was the young man. The people who ignored the old woman's need probably felt worse by withholding help, even though they thought not getting involved would make them feel better. However, according to research on benevolence, the young man probably felt a surge of happiness. Even though it was inconvenient for him to stop and help the old woman, his feeling of being inconvenienced was most certainly overshadowed by the warm and happy feeling of helping someone.

The Iroquois Indians refer to this as "the benevolent desire of the soul." The human soul has a need to do good for others and when that need is expressed, the payment one receives is happiness. Unfortunately, many people ignore the benevolent desire of their souls and, as a result, they walk away from the happiness buffet with an empty plate.

In my opinion, the happiness boost we get from helping others is proof of a wonderful spiritual plan. It works like this:

- There will always be people in need.
- Happiness is the one thing everyone wants.
- People who help others feel happier.
- Therefore, the system is designed for people to get the help they need, because the ones offering assistance will receive a rush of the one thing they want more than anything—happiness.

As more people begin to understand that helping others is a gift of happiness they give to themselves, the needs of more and more people will be met.

By witnessing what happened that afternoon in Albuquerque, I experienced secondhand happiness. A person watching someone perform a magnanimous gesture will feel an increased level of happiness as well.

So, a person being kind feels happier and a person watching someone being kind also feels happier. And we know that the person receiving the kindness feels happier. Therefore, to make not only ourselves happier but also at least one other person (and possibly more if they are fortunate to observe our kindness), we should do something nice for someone every day with no expectation of reciprocity.

Simply finding something—*anything*—that you can do to help someone else will make you feel happier. If you set a goal each day to find some way of helping someone, your happiness level will increase.

Here's how a Chinese saying puts it:

If you want happiness for an hour, take a nap.
If you want happiness for a day, go fishing.
If you want happiness for a month, get married.
If you want happiness for a year, inherit a fortune.
If you want happiness for a lifetime, help someone else.

There are thousands of ways to do this, and you will discover them if you look for them. Let someone in ahead of you in traffic, hold a door for someone, offer to help carry something for someone, listen to someone who needs to share, pay for the meal of the person behind you at the drive-thru, give someone a compliment. Anything that is done with a sincere desire to make someone else's day better creates a halo effect of happiness in your own life.

Putting It to the Test

I decided to put this to the test and, in the process, I discovered a way to magnify the impact of a kind act. I call this "The Combo."

Every Thursday morning, I get together with three friends at a local restaurant to share what is going on in our lives and to pray affirmatively for one another.

I happened to notice that a group of a dozen or so elderly women gather at the same restaurant at about the same time as my group, talking and praying together as well. Neither my friends nor I know any of these women personally, but we always acknowledge one another with warm smiles.

I decided to pay for breakfast for each of the women as a test to see if doing so made me feel happier. I opted to do this anonymously so that I could observe their reactions and to lessen any qualms they may have that about receiving something from a stranger.

The following Thursday morning I arrived early and asked to speak to the restaurant manager. A smiling but haggard woman in a manager's uniform approached. I pulled her aside and told her that I had seen these ladies each week and that I wanted to surreptitiously do something nice for them.

I asked her to tell each of the ladies to order anything they wanted and to inform them that an anonymous friend would be paying for their meal. She told me this would be simple to do, because she has seen these women every Thursday for several years and knows each of them on sight. I gave the manager my debit card number to charge for the ladies' meals and sat down to wait for my friends.

As each of the elderly women passed by my table carrying their muffins and coffee, I felt truly happy for having done something nice. Later, as I was about to leave, I flagged down the store manager to thank her.

The manager looked at me with shock and embarrassment. "I'm so sorry!" she blurted. "We had an emergency in the kitchen and I had to stay in the back helping out. I completely forgot to tell the cashiers about our little plan. So, the ladies actually paid for their own food and drinks."

After a second's disappointment, I realized that just the idea that I had done something nice for someone had filled me with happiness for more than an hour. My happiness level had easily jumped from an 8 to a 10 for the entire time I had sat watching the ladies eat and talk to one another, even though I had not paid for them as planned.

"I understand," I said smiling to the manager. "It's no big deal."

"How about this?" I continued. "Those ladies come in every week at the same time. Let's do it *next* Thursday."

After apologizing again, the manager promised she would make it happen. "I swear to you that we will do it next week," she said. "No matter what!"

Over the next seven days, I found myself anticipating the upcoming Thursday morning. My mind would frequently fantasize about how surprised and happy these ladies were going to be when they discovered that an anonymous benefactor was paying for their breakfast. More significant, I discovered that I was much happier whenever I anticipated this good deed yet to come.

True to her word, the manager personally worked the counter the following Thursday, motioning over the women from the group to her register. After each of them placed her order, the manager said that a friend who wished to remain anonymous was paying for her breakfast.

I sat and watched as the ladies all walked by carrying their trays with big smiles on their faces. I found that I needed to drop my head and watch them with my peripheral vision, because it was clear that they were scanning the restaurant trying to figure out who had done such a nice thing.

Even though our usual booth was several tables removed from where the ladies always sat, I overheard them speaking excitedly about their good fortune.

My happiness was palpable. My friends sensed my joy and asked me what was going on. When I told them, I could see that they, too, had become significantly happier for being so close to a generous act.

Paying for the women's breakfasts cost me about $60. For sixty bucks, I had made myself and about 15 other people significantly happier, including the restaurant manager. Although she is always friendly, that morning the manager had beamed with joy for being a part of this act of generosity.

In *The How of Happiness*, Sonja Lyubomirsky writes that people find joy in doing something nice for other people. In *Stumbling on Happiness*, Harvard psychology professor Dan Gilbert cites research showing that people tend to enjoy something more if they have time to anticipate it first. Offering to buy someone a delicious meal results in far greater enjoyment if the meal is a few days off in the future.

Thanks to the snafu the previous week at the restaurant, I had unwittingly linked these two happiness-inducing activities—benevolence and anticipation—together. I found that doing something nice for someone made me happy for a moment—but *anticipating doing something nice* for someone made me equally as happy, but for all the moments leading up to the actual experience. This compounded and extended the happiness I gained.

The Combo Formula

What I like to call "The Combo" is the combination of a good deed multiplied by the anticipation of the good deed. The formula is:

$$\textbf{Good Deed} \times \textbf{Anticipation} = \textbf{Happiness}^2$$

A very powerful action to stimulate a higher and lasting level of happiness is to make a commitment every morning to find someone to do something nice for that day. Setting this intention assures you that an opportunity to do something magnanimous will present itself. I have found that when this happens, I get downright giddy thinking, "Here it is! I get to do my good deed for the day, and feeling happier will be my reward!"

Ralph Waldo Emerson is believed to have said, "Happiness is a perfume which you cannot pour on someone without getting some on yourself." When you do something nice for someone else, it not only makes that person happy but it makes you happy as well. And when you combine an act of kindness with the anticipation of performing the act of kindness, you create a powerful happiness combo!

WISHING WELL

A common practice in many countries around the world is to make a wish and throw coins into a well—hence the term "wishing well."

This is actually an ancient ritual. Because of the life-sustaining power of water, people thousands of years ago in arid lands thought that wells were actually portholes to the realm of the gods. Their belief was that if someone desired something a great deal, they should make an offering by throwing something of value into a well to court divine favor.

Your wish is to be a happier person. For your wish to be granted, you are going to have to make an offering—an offering that might be quite a struggle at first. But over time it gets easier. To be fully liberated from discontent and misery and, thereby, free yourself to be happy, this is an offering you are going to have to make.

You are going to have to offer the right to be happy to everyone.

Everyone.

The people you disagree with, the people you feel have hurt you, the people who have betrayed you, the people you feel don't deserve happiness—you have to be willing to see all of them happy.

British philosopher Bertrand Russell wrote, "Contempt for happiness is usually contempt for other people's happiness." To feel that another person does not deserve happiness is a violation of spiritual law. Because we are all of one spirit, whatever you deny others, you simultaneously deny yourself.

You can't be happy and carry around anger and resentment toward other people. One of the most powerful prayers you can make is to pray for another person's happiness—especially someone you feel doesn't deserve it.

Learning This Lesson Myself

In 2005, I became the minister of a church in Kansas City. This church had been around for 47 years with only three other ministers serving as spiritual leader during that time. It might seem like the church was on solid footing and that there was very little turnover. However, the founding minister had served for 40 of those 47 years and, during the next 7 years, the church had gone through two ministers.

I soon encountered a cancerous undercurrent of fear, negativity, and discontent that pervaded the church.

In October 2010, many of the same people who had ousted the previous minister banded together insisting that I also leave. People who had not attended services in years began to show up on Sunday mornings circulating petitions demanding that I be fired.

Angry calls came to my home, and I received nasty letters and emails. One man even approached my precious teenage daughter saying, "Tell your father to quit. We don't want him here anymore." This broke her heart, and when she told me, I burned with hurt and anger.

At the end of the service each week, a handful of people would come through the "hug line"—the line at the end of service where people could have a moment to speak to the minister—and they'd wrap their arms around me, all the while whispering threats and hate-filled comments into my ears.

I endured this for three months. As 2011 approached, I realized that this mob's determination to get me out at any cost was not going to abate. I was exhausted—physically, emotionally, and spiritually. I called Don Perry, my good friend and the president of my board, and told him I was leaving.

For several months, I stayed at home, raw from the experience. I felt angry, resentful, and disillusioned. Mostly, I grieved for the many wonderful people who had been collateral damage in the scorching attacks that came my way.

On a scale of 1 to 10, my happiness level rarely peaked above a 2 for several months.

Finding the Gift

In *Illusions*, author Richard Bach wrote, "There is no such thing as a problem without a gift for you in its hands." And it was during this time that a wonderful gift came into my life. From the depths of despair I made a resolution to become happy.

I vowed not to be just as happy as I had been previously, but to significantly and sustainably surpass my previous happiness level. I began my study of happiness and to experiment with my own life. The result of this journey is the book you now hold in your hands.

Over the next year, I began to master my thoughts and my words. I found that I was in control of my level of happiness and I strove to increase my happiness a little each week.

But like the school buses we discussed in the introduction to this book, there was a governor device keeping me from accelerating—to higher levels of happiness.

Although I had become a much happier person, whenever someone mentioned one of the antagonists from the church—or if I ran into one of them at a store or if I saw a post about one of them on Facebook—my happiness crashed to the ground.

It felt as if my heart was a heavy iron gate that slammed shut whenever any reference was made to any of these people. More than a year had passed, yet these angry people still held the controls on my "Happystat." Resolving to regain this control, I began to pray affirmatively for them one by one, a method I discussed in Chapter 5.

My ego had convinced me that I was right and that they were wrong. However, one day in meditation I realized that although in my mind I was right, in their minds *they* were right. I had to climb down from my fortress of being right and begin to desire that these people be happy.

I began to sit each morning and call them to mind one by one. I **A**cknowledged the person's oneness with God. I **C**laimed health, happiness, and prosperity for this person, and then I gave **T**hanks for them living a happy and fulfilling life. Further, I began to give thanks for the gift they had given me. I had discovered both a level of strength and happiness within myself that I never knew existed.

At first, affirming these people's happiness and expressing gratitude for them was extremely difficult. Saying these prayers aloud felt like chewing on broken glass. However, it became easier and easier over time.

Liberating the Soul to Be Happy

In Matthew 5:43–46, Jesus states, "You have heard that it was said, 'Love your neighbor and hate your enemy.' But I tell you, love your enemies and pray for those who persecute you, that you may be children of your Father in heaven. He causes his sun to rise on the evil and the good, and sends rain on the righteous and the unrighteous. If you love those who love you, what reward will you get?"

Praying for those who have hurt, tormented, or persecuted you is not something you do to appease God or to get God on your side. As Wayne Dyer observed, God created a round planet without sides. Praying for and wanting others to be happy *frees your own soul to be happy.*

Confucius said, "To be wronged is nothing unless you continue to remember it." If you continue to exhume and ruminate over others' misdeeds toward you, you will fester with hatred and resentment and you cannot be happy. To be happy, you have to wish other people well and truly mean it.

Early twentieth-century theologian Harry Emerson Fosdick put it succinctly: "Hating people is like burning down your own house to get rid of a rat." The negative energy that boils within you dissolves any chance you have at true happiness.

You can be no closer to God than the person farthest from your heart. You can do all the other things that induce a feeling of happiness. You can smile, speak affirmatively, engage in kind acts, and more, but if you are holding hatred toward another human being, your happiness structure is built upon a rotten foundation. It will come crashing down at some point.

It's been said that, "For every minute you are angry you lose sixty seconds of happiness." Certainly there are people who, in their fear and ignorance, have hurt you in the past, but if that is limiting your current happiness, *they* are not hurting you now, *you* are hurting yourself. Continuing to be angry at these people robs you of fully realizing happiness.

Again, think of a person who is truly happy. Better yet, look at the box top of the happy life you are assembling one puzzle piece at a time. If you are honest, you will see there is no room for anger and resentment in a truly happy life.

Forgiveness Doesn't Necessarily Mean Reconciliation

Wishing someone well can be done from a distance. If there is someone who habitually treats you harshly, you should wish that person well and create a mental picture of that person being happy, and then hold that vision until it becomes comfortable for you. This will open the spigot of happiness so it can flow to you. But you don't have to invite that person to dinner or allow him or her back into your life.

There is another sound and practical reason for affirming the happiness of those who have hurt you. In her novel *Kushiel's Dart*, author Jacqueline Carey put it well: "It is my observation, though, that happiness limits the amount of suffering one is willing to inflict upon others."

Happy people tend to be kind. Unkind people tend to be unhappy.

A Course in Miracles, the guide to spiritual transformation, says, "Those who see themselves as whole make no demands." A happy person is a person who feels whole and complete. They are unlikely therefore to make demands of others or to do them harm.

People Who Are Hurting Hurt People

People who hurt you are themselves hurting. If they have not worked to heal their pain, there is a good chance that they will attempt to displace their own suffering by hurting you. Wish them well, but keep your distance.

I do not believe the people from the church who attacked me were happy people. Similarly, the people who have hurt you are not happy people. The happier someone is, the less likely he or she is to harm anyone. This compassionate understanding is motivation enough for us to wish them well and affirm their happiness!

RECAPPING "ACTIONS OF HAPPINESS"

- Put yourself on a positivity diet. Listen to only upbeat and inspiring songs and watch positive TV shows and movies.

- Take the "expressway to happiness." Express what you are grateful for with a gratitude journal and speak aloud what you are grateful for throughout the day.

- Focus on the box top of your life. Invest a minute or so each morning to review your vision of yourself living a happy life.

- Make a plan every morning to do something nice for someone. Remember:

Good Deed × Anticipation = Happiness^2

- Wish everyone well. Affirm happiness for everyone, *especially* those you feel don't deserve it.

PART THREE

Living Happiness

When I let go of what I am, I become what I might be.
—Lao-tzu

CHAPTER SIX

Habits of Happiness

Happiness is a habit – cultivate it.
—Elbert Hubbard

"C'mon, get up!" my father exclaimed. "Today's the day we start running."

I slid one eye open and saw my father standing next to my bed. His hair was a tangled mess, his chin was covered in stubble, and he was wearing a new powder-blue running suit. I groaned and rolled over, turning my back toward him.

"Tomorrow," I croaked.

"No, today!" my father said as he jerked the covers off me in one swift motion.

"But I'm *tired*," I whined. "I was up late studying for a science test. I promise we'll start tomorrow."

"No," my father said sternly. "Get up. . .now! I'll meet you outside in five minutes."

After he left the room, I muttered some words that he would have punished me for saying had he heard them. I dug through my drawer looking for something I could wear to stave off the November cold. I searched through my dresser until I found a pair of athletic socks and then I rummaged through the floor of my closet in search of sneakers.

"Let's go. . .*now!*" my father barked as he tapped impatiently on my window from outside.

I laced up my shoes, grumbling all the while, and stomped out of my room, through the kitchen, across the porch, and down the stairs to where he stood.

"On you mark, get set, go!" my father said, and the two of us began jogging slowly up the gravel road. The road was only about two hundred feet long, but I began puffing heavily less than halfway.

I was 17. My father was 47. I was 100 pounds overweight. My father was skinny, but had not exercised since leaving the Navy more than two decades earlier.

We ran in silence; the only sounds were our labored breathing and the crunch of our shoes on the gravel road. Soon, I felt like someone had jammed a screwdriver into my left side, and my body listed to the left. The pain threw off my pace and I gasped for breath.

We reached the end of the road and I asked, "Okay. . .(gasp). . . now. . .(gasp). . .what?"

My father looked left and right at the intersecting blacktop street. I could tell by his expression that he had not thought through our next steps.

It was 1976, and the jogging craze had been in full swing for several years. We were late arrivals to the party and I began to understand why jogging was called a "craze." Running for the sake of running seemed totally crazy to me.

Sidestepping the decision as to which direction to take, my dad said, "Let's just jog in place right here."

"Jog in place?" I asked with a sarcastic tone only a teenager can manage. "For how long?"

My father didn't answer, and I could tell by the look on his face that he was growing tired of my questions and my sullen teenage attitude. We jogged in one spot for a couple of minutes that felt like an eternity. Then, without a word he turned back up the gravel road toward home and I followed; the cold air caused my eyes to tear and my lungs to wheeze.

When we arrived at our house, he and I both collapsed onto the stairs.

"There!" he shouted. "Don't you feel better?"

"Absolutely!" I lied.

We went inside. He poured himself a cup of coffee while I went to my room to shower and get dressed for school. The following morning the scenario repeated, but in reverse.

Standing next to his bed I said, "Dad! C'mon, get up. We're supposed to go jogging."

"I'm too tired," he growled.

"We said we would do this every day," I reminded him.

"My legs hurt from running yesterday," he said, pulling the covers up over his head.

"My legs hurt, too," I said. "C'mon, get up."

He ignored me.

"Dad!" I screamed.

No response.

I was dressed and ready and felt irritated that he wasn't going to get up and join me. For the second morning in a row, I stomped through the house, this time angry that the person who had gotten me into this jogging nonsense had already quit on me.

I decided to jog by myself. I stood at the foot of the stairs for a few minutes trying to psyche myself up as I watched my breath turn to mist in the cool morning air.

Just as I was taking my first steps, from over my shoulder I heard the door slam and my father's voice. "All right, all right," he said. "Let's do this, then." His voice sounded more resigned than resolute.

That morning's run was identical to the one the day before–a couple of hundred feet up the gravel road, a few minutes of jogging in place, then a shuffling jog back.

That was the last time my father and I ever ran together. The following morning, I lay in bed waiting for him to come and get me and he, likewise, waited for me to come and get him. Neither of us had sufficiently enjoyed or benefited from our two brief runs, and we were both fine with never repeating the process again.

Running did not become a habit for us. Five years later, however, I took up jogging again. This time running did become a habit for me and I ran every day for two decades. I still include running as part of my exercise regimen.

Directing the Current of Habit

What was missing when my father and I ran together? Why didn't running become habitual for us?

Habit is a strong current that carries us along without our even being aware of its power or influence. You have habitual ways of eating, dressing, driving, working, talking, and relaxing. You have a habitual morning routine, you drive to work along a habitual route, and you tend to habitually buy the same items and brands at the grocery store. Most of what human beings do is habitual.

If we could harness the power of habit, we could revamp our lives. However, our current habits are strong, and it takes effort to reshape them into new ones.

Changing your thoughts, words, and actions can increase your happiness level, but over time you will settle back to your typical happiness level if you don't develop new happiness habits.

Our goal is to make your new, higher happiness level your default, so that regardless of what transpires you don't dip below this set point too deeply or for very long. By making your happiness highs last longer and shortening the extent and duration of your lows, you will feel happier overall. Consciously forming new habits puts the process of increased happiness on autopilot.

In his book *The Power of Habit*, Charles Duhigg explains that there are three major components to creating a habit:

1. Cues
2. Routines
3. Rewards

These three components reinforce one another, creating what Duhigg calls a "habit loop."

First, we experience a cue or trigger; we then engage in a routine; and if the routine results in a reward, a pattern for responding to similar cues in the future is created.

When cues, routines, and rewards are combined, human beings develop a craving, and it is these cravings that give habits their force and staying power.

When it came to running, my father cued me to get up, get dressed, and get going. The following day I cued him. On both days we then engaged in the routine of jogging. However, we never experienced a reward for our actions, so our brains never experienced a craving.

This is why most New Year's resolutions fail. Consider that list of the most common New Year's resolutions from the *USA. gov* website:

- Drink less alcohol.
- Eat healthy food.
- Get a better education.
- Get a better job.
- Get fit.
- Lose weight.
- Manage debt.
- Manage stress.
- Quit smoking.
- Reduce, reuse, and recycle.
- Save money.
- Take a trip.
- Volunteer to help others.

Did you notice something?

These resolutions are all routines. Yet they are unclear as to cues, they all require effort, and they don't fully convey true rewards. When cues are missed, old habits kick in. Attempting routines without the promise of rewards is taxing and uninspiring.

The Lure of Craving

When I began to run in earnest, I lived in downtown Wilmington, North Carolina, one of the most beautiful and historic cities in the United States. It was a major struggle to get up early every morning and put on my running shoes, but I was new to the city and committed to making each run an exploration of a different part of the city.

I began to sleep in my running shorts and T-shirt to cue myself. I also kept my running shoes next to the bed with my socks on top of the shoes.

As I ran the sidewalks alongside Wilmington's cobblestone streets, I reveled in the beauty of the antebellum homes and their well-maintained gardens. This was my reward for engaging in the routine of running.

After about three consecutive weeks of daily runs, I realized that running had become a habit. It was simply a part of who I was. I didn't have to think about running, it was no longer a hassle; it actually became something I looked forward to. However, I realized that I had seen all of the beautiful homes repeatedly and it was no longer this that motivated me.

If the appeal of Wilmington's beauty no longer inspired me, what was it that had converted running from a daily grind into a habit?

I discovered the answer when I missed two days of running in a row. The first day I had an early morning meeting and the next day it poured rain. By the end of the second day I felt lethargic, listless, and irritable.

Running each day had given me a series of rewards I had not fully realized, and I sorely missed them after two days of not jogging. Running caused my body to release endorphins and it increased my metabolism, causing me to feel more energetic and upbeat. I felt less stressed throughout the day and my mood was elevated for longer periods of time. I noticed that when I walked, my body felt more comfortable and, after only a few of weeks of running, I was in better shape. I even noticed that my clothes fit better.

Running may have been a struggle for 30 minutes each morning, but for the rest of the day I felt great. When I didn't run, I saved the 30 minutes of hassle but I lost out on the many pleasurable outcomes that came throughout the rest of the day. Rewards build cravings, which cause us to adopt new routines to cues.

CUES

Twenty years later, my girlfriend and I held hands as we meandered slowly past the white tents that served as booths for the Plaza Arts Festival in Kansas City. It was a cool evening, and the air was alive with the energy of thousands of art enthusiasts. On our left there were captivating black-and-white photos. On our right we saw striking acrylic paintings of cityscapes. Ahead, an artist sold tall, rough-hewn sculptures of sunflowers.

We walked for several hundred yards, stopping here and there to admire various pieces of art and to comment on which ones we might like to purchase someday.

"I'm hungry," I said, placing one hand on my stomach.

"No, you're not," my sweetheart responded, squeezing my other hand.

"Yes, I'm hungry," I said, squeezing her hand even more tightly.

"No," she replied. "You're not."

"Look," I said a bit peevishly, "I should know whether I'm hungry or not."

"Actually, you really don't know yourself very well," she replied with a disarming smile.

"What do you mean?" I asked.

"Smell," she said.

Taking a deep breath in through my nose I said, "Yeah. . .so?"

"So, what do you smell?" she asked.

"Mmmmm. . .food!" I said. "Big soft pretzels and fresh popcorn and candied pecans and—"

"Exactly," she said. "You're not hungry. You're just smelling food, and you equated that with feeling hungry."

"But I really do feel hungry," I said.

She pulled me toward her and looked deeply into my eyes. "I don't doubt that you think you feel hungry," she said. "It's just your body giving you a sensation to justify your wanting to eat the food you smell."

I thought about this and she continued. "You weren't hungry when we were at the other end of the arts fair were you?"

"Well. . .no. I guess not," I said.

"But right now, in the middle of the food vendors, you're hungry all of a sudden?" she asked.

"Maybe you have a point," I said.

I resolved to hold off eating anything for 10 minutes. If I was still hungry after that, I would come back for something. Later that night, as I prepared for bed, I realized that I hadn't gone back for a snack at the arts festival. In fact, I got so caught up in the exhibits and our time together that I even forgot to eat dinner. Obviously, I had not been hungry. I had been triggered to eat by the smell of food and reacted habitually.

Trigger (Food Smell) + Habitual Routine
(Eating) + Reward (Food) = Craving

As with all habits, the trigger and the reward get linked when the craving is solidified, and then the routine becomes automatic.

When it comes to happiness, you are constantly being triggered. Thousands of little cues occur each day that you can choose to let affect your mood positively or negatively.

When a trigger occurs, you often react—note that I didn't say *respond*—because a response entails thoughtful action. No, you react habitually based on previous behaviors that have brought you rewards in the past.

"But what if I react negatively?" you may wonder. "If something cues me, why would I choose to think, say, or do something that is going to make me feel less happy? How could being unhappy lead to a reward?"

Here are some of the rewards we get for choosing a lower level of happiness. We aren't typically aware of them, but we can begin to crave them, thereby reinforcing negative routines.

Attention

Let's consider a fictitious example. Let's presume that your doctor tells you that she has found something irregular in your blood work and wants to do a few more tests to make sure that you're all right.

"What is it?" you ask.

"Probably nothing," she says.

"But, what *could* it be?" you ask gravely.

"Well, like I say, it's probably nothing," she says. "But it could be anything from just a little anemia to. . ."

"To what?"

"Well, it's highly unlikely, but it might even be leukemia. But I'm pretty certain that's not the case."

"Leukemia?" you say, visibly shaken.

"Very, very slight chance of that," she says. "We'll run some more tests and we'll know for sure."

As you leave the doctor's office, you dial your cell phone.

"Mom," you say, stifling a tear. "My doctor thinks I might have leukemia."

"What?" your mother shrieks. "What did the doctor say?"

"She found something unusual in my blood work. I'm coming back next week for more tests. She said it could be leukemia."

"My poor baby," your mother says. "I'm getting on a plane and coming to see you right away!"

"Oh, Mom, don't bother," you say.

"No!" your mother counters. "I'll be there first thing tomorrow."

Clicking the "end" button on your phone, your mind begins to plow through lists of other friends and family you might call who will give you the attention you secretly crave.

In this case, the cue is the doctor telling you that your blood tests came back with some irregularities. When you pressed her, she said that it was probably nothing but that it could be *anything* from anemia to leukemia, although it was highly unlikely to be leukemia.

In truth, the doctor gave you neutral information. However, you know that the surest way to get attention from your family and some of your friends is to have a problem. The bigger the problem is, the more the attention.

I know this routine well. My own mother was a very loving woman who always came through when things were difficult.

She loved to be needed and to help other people, and this is why she excelled in her career as a nurse.

For decades I called my mom every Sunday night to catch up. I discovered that if I had good news, she would say, "Oh, that's great, darling." And that would be the end of it.

However, if I had a problem, my mother would express concern and offer support. We would then talk at length about the situation. I found myself going through my week looking for problems and difficulties to share with my mother that upcoming Sunday evening. The unrealized intention of looking for the worst experiences in my life and amplifying them when I talked to her decreased my level of happiness, but it provided me with more attention from my mother.

Many people will unconsciously root through their minds while driving to visit a friend to think of problems to share, because they feel that sharing their woes will make certain they receive the maximum amount of attention from the other person.

Pain Addiction

As we've discussed, most people live in what Eckhart Tolle calls a pain-body. Psychologists are now beginning to give the pain-body concept a more clinical diagnosis: *pain addiction.*

When a person worries or frets about something, the body responds to this emotional pain and squirts a little shot of endorphins into his or her bloodstream. In other words, choosing to go emotionally low actually gets the person a little high.

In reality, the endorphin kick only brings the person back up to his or her predominant happiness setting, but the reward of the jolt of endogenous morphine reinforces the habit of being less happy than one otherwise might be.

When pain addicts experience a cue that might induce an increase in happiness, such as receiving a compliment or finding $20 on the street, they can feel anxious because their predominant way of thinking about themselves is threatened. This is all unconscious and automatic. They will then begin to worry about losing the money, or whether the praise they received was genuine. Or, they may ruminate over something else upsetting—anything they can do to feed their addiction to emotional pain.

These people may not be happy, but they are comfortable in their unhappiness and if they begin to feel too happy, their bodies will shut off their internal morphine drip and they will go into withdrawal.

If you are a pain addict, what you'll discover is that becoming happier may, at first, make you feel a little anxious. Over time, however, you will begin to enjoy a more enduring emotional high without the slingshot of the emotional lows to take you there.

Reinforcement of the Fantasy Bond

Changing how you view yourself and your place in your world is not easy.

The essence of the fantasy bond is that there is something wrong with you—a belief that you are inherently flawed. This belief supports the omniscience of "God"—in this case, your own emotionally wounded parents, who were incapable of giving you the love and acceptance you deserved.

When a neutral cue occurs, you may choose to feel unhappy, because being unhappy is "what you deserve." As a result, you may experience less happiness—but the reward is that somewhere at a very deep level you feel, as poet Robert Browning put it, "God's in His heaven—All's right with the world!"

The world may be dark, scary, and unappealing, but it feels like home.

When faced with an opportunity to feel happy, a person tied to the fantasy bond will experience a flip of that Upper Limit switch Gay Hendricks writes about. "Everything is going really well," this person subconsciously realizes, but then concludes, "There is something very wrong here."

This person will begin to think, say, or do something to bring things back down to what he or she considers to be an acceptable level of happiness. The person then feels rewarded because the world is once again spinning as it should.

Ego Pacification

Until one learns to put that Sacred Clown of a rude roommate in its place, the ego will attack at every turn—most typically when things are going well. When you start feeling happier, the ego begins to freak out, because it senses that its control over you is eroding.

I have a good friend who suffers from tinnitus, which is the medical term for incessant ringing or buzzing in the ears. Many people experience this phenomenon from time to time. We seem to hear something in our heads that can range from subtle white noise to a high-pitched squeal. For most people the irritating sound goes away over time, but for people who have tinnitus, the noise never stops.

The ego voice in our minds is much like tinnitus, and when you first begin to become a happier person, it will turn up the volume of its negative chatter. If you continue with the practices we've covered thus far to control happy thoughts, words, and actions—especially those designed to assert dominance over the ego—it will abate. However, this takes some time, and in the short term, it can actually increase periodically.

When you first begin your happiness journey, the ego may begin to buzz in your mind like a swarm of angry bees, because it feels justifiably threatened. To appease the ego, you might choose to focus on negative and unpleasant things. The price you pay is diminished happiness. The reward you receive is less negative chatter and assaults from your ego.

These are just some of the reasons your happiness level is not at the level it could be. Later in this chapter, you'll discover positive rewards that will far exceed these negative ones and you'll be able to focus on them to sweep these happiness-limiting rewards aside.

In *The Analects*, Confucius states, "Men's natures are alike; it is their habits that separate them." Life's challenges trigger everyone every day. Changing you reactions to cues and actively creating new ones will separate you from the preponderance of habitually unhappy people.

Look for Ways to Create New Cues

Here are a few ideas:

- Change your alarm clock setting so that, rather than being awakened to the distressing reports of a "news" channel or a jarring alert, you hear an upbeat and inspiring song instead. (My current wake-up song is "H.A.P.P.Y. Radio" by Edwin Starr.) Whatever you hear first thing as you awaken becomes a soundtrack for your morning. As the song runs through your mind, you will feel the emotions it inspires, so choose wisely.

- Change your Internet home page from Yahoo! News or CNN to a page that provides good news or a daily inspirational thought or video.

- Change your lunch companions to people who are happy and upbeat; as you nourish your body by eating lunch, you will also nourish your mood by being with positive people.

- Change the ringtone on your phone to one that expresses how great and happy you want your life to be. (My current ringtone is "The Future's So Bright, I Gotta Wear Shades" by Timbuk3.)

- If you have an acquaintance who loves to share upsetting information with you via email, create a special folder into which this person's emails will be sent when they arrive. And then, don't read them!

In addition to choosing new cues, you can work to alter your reactions to existing cues:

- When a challenging situation arises, call someone who will provide positive views, hope, and support, rather than someone who will respond with negativity, excuses, and commiseration.

- When someone is rude or challenging, strive to see him or her as a person who has gone through something painful or difficult that caused his or her reaction. The Buddha had a wise suggestion for times when one is confronted with a difficult person. He recommended that his followers visualize the challenging individual as an infant and then spend several moments imagining that they are holding the infant as they pretend that he or she is their own precious child.

- Put problems into perspective. The problem that you are concerned about today will be tomorrow's nonissue. Every day has problems; release them to the Spirit and have faith that they will be resolved.

- Whenever a problem arises, force yourself to come up with three ways this situation might actually work out in your favor over time.

One of the more interesting routines to alter an existing cue was practiced by my grandparents and many people of their generation living in the southeastern United States. Knowing the happiness-inducing power of releasing negative emotions about other people, it was commonplace for these people to name a new dog after a despised relative who had died.

When the family would get a new puppy, they would gather together to discuss who was the most disliked deceased relative. They would then name the puppy after that person.

Let's say, for example, that before his passing Ole Uncle George was a mean-spirited and argumentative guy and that the members of the family still harbored negative feelings toward him. The new puppy would be named "George," because few things are more cute than a puppy or more loving and loyal than a dog. Therefore, a new emotional response was formed around the cue of his name. When the name George came up, it became linked to the family dog rather than the irritating old uncle.

Developing new cues as well as new routines to old cues requires an intention and taking action. Soon the new triggers will launch whole new routines and rewards leading to a craving for more positive mental habits, which then become self-sustaining.

ROUTINES

Before his retirement, Bill Watterson brilliantly interwove social commentary, profound insights, childhood innocence, and just plain fun into his daily *Calvin and Hobbes* cartoon strip.

In one of my favorites, Calvin inserts a quarter into a gumball machine and to his amazement and delight receives not one but *two* gumballs.

"Yowza!" Calvin shouts as he begins to dance about, excitedly pumping his arms in the air. Calvin tells anyone within earshot about his good fortune. "I *love* this gumball machine!" he says. "What a *great* gumball machine!"

After several moments of this victory dance, another kid walks by and Calvin brags, "This machine gave me two gumballs for a quarter!" The other child replies, "It must be broken. . .you should have gotten three."

Crestfallen, Calvin glares at the gumball machine and mumbles, "Stupid gumball machine."

The cue may have been Calvin's receiving one, two, or three gumballs, but it was his expectation that contextualized this trigger. When he expected one gumball and got two, he was significantly happier. When he found out that he should have gotten three and received only two gumballs, his happiness dipped precipitously. Our expectations dictate how we will interpret a cue and what routine our thoughts, words, and actions will take as a result.

The Impact of Expectations

When I was in Tanzania helping to build a birthing center at a hospital in Mwanza, the roads in that country bewildered me. Most of the side roads are made of dirt and strewn with large boulders that drivers must weave around. It is impossible to drive on these roads without veering sharply to one side and then the other.

The highways are paved, but they, too, present challenges. It is legal to drive at speeds of 55 to 70 miles per hour, but doing so for a sustained period of time is impossible.

The police in Tanzania don't own cars. You will often see them in their crisp white uniforms standing on the side of the highway. With a white-gloved hand, an officer will motion a driver to pull over to the side of the road *not* to cite the driver for an infraction but because the cop needs a ride down the highway.

The lack of police vehicles has inspired the Tanzanian government to come up with a unique way of keeping speeders in check. There are raised speed bumps spaced approximately one mile apart along all highways. A trip of one hundred miles involves slowing down to 5 miles per hour approximately one hundred times along the way.

Tanzanian side roads are barely navigable, and the highways require constant deceleration and acceleration. In addition to those physical challenges, there are bicycles, oxen, and mobs of pedestrians that constantly weave in and out of traffic. And yet, Tanzanian drivers don't complain about these conditions.

Why? Because this setup is all Tanzanians know of what it means to drive. If these conditions were suddenly the norm in the United States, Great Britain, China, or any other industrialized country, drivers would be frustrated to the point of hysteria. Tanzanian drivers have no expectation of better conditions and therefore are unaffected by the driving challenges.

Remember that our definition of happiness is more akin to contentment than to bliss or joy. We should be aware that our expectations—be they to receive three gumballs for one quarter or to drive along a road unencumbered by obstacles—dictate how we evaluate our lives and how we respond to the cues and triggers that occur.

Thus far we have looked at several routines that will increase your level of happiness:

- Claiming that you are a happy person.
- Setting a happiness goal and measuring your progress .
- Separating from your ego by giving it a distinct voice, and through regular meditation.
- Seeing challenging people as Sacred Clowns who are in your life to help you discover latent resources of happiness and compassion.
- Keeping what you say positive and practicing affirmative prayer.
- Taking in only positive mental nutrition.
- Making a gratitude list and reminding yourself constantly of the things you have to be grateful for.
- Planning and doing good deeds for other people.
- Reviewing often, and in vivid detail, what your life will be like as you become happier.
- Affirming happiness for others, especially those you feel have harmed you.

Below are a couple more routines that you can practice when life triggers you.

Practice Your ABCDs

In Greek mythology, Sisyphus was a king cursed to forever roll an immense boulder up a hill—only to watch helplessly as it rolled back down again.

Despite your best efforts, it may feel like you are a modern-day incarnation of Sisyphus, rolling your happiness level up the hill only to be triggered by a life experience that leaves you standing and watching as the boulder rolls back down and takes your happiness with it.

Of all of the techniques developed by learned psychologists and researchers for the purpose of shifting a person from negative rumination to a positive, happier focus, the following is one of the most powerful and practical.

Developed by Martin Seligman, this process not only helps you keep your happiness level high but also follows the model of habit formation we've been discussing, and so the practice becomes habitual rather quickly. Seligman calls this "the ABCD method," and it works like this: Whenever something cues you and you feel your happiness boulder starting to slip down the hill, grab a pen and a piece of paper and write.

Adversity: *Identify what adverse circumstance occurred. In one sentence specify what triggered you.*

EXAMPLE: "I called Edwin three days ago and he hasn't called me back."

Belief: *Write down what you believe resulted from what happened. You have a habitual routine for believing why experiences like this happen. Write out your beliefs uncensored, giving your fearful ego its say.*

EXAMPLE:
- "Edwin has decided he doesn't like me anymore."

- "He doesn't want to be my friend."
- "He's found someone else he would rather spend time with."
- "People always leave me once they get to know me."

Consequences: What are the consequences of having this belief? Give words to the feelings you are experiencing. This is a time for honesty and to let your upset flow.

EXAMPLE:
- "I feel sad."
- "I feel worthless."
- "I feel ignored."
- "I feel lonely."
- "I feel unimportant."
- "I feel abandoned."
- "I'm frightened that I'll never have another close friend like him."

Disputation: Now it's time to write a new story. Just as my daughter, Lia, did when her boyfriend didn't text her back, begin to list all of the things that might have caused this cue instead of the dire scenarios you have been creating in your mind.

EXAMPLE:
- "It's only been three days. I remember it once took him a week to call me back but he *did* call me!"

- "I'm sure he's just busy."
- "Edwin may have an emergency that has kept him from calling."
- "He may be sick."
- "He may have lost his phone."
- "Someone in his family may be sick and he's been too busy to return my call."
- "Something may have gone wrong with his voice mail and he didn't get my message."

When I first discovered this technique, I found it so helpful that I began to carry a journal with me everywhere I went.

Each time I was triggered by a negative occurrence and followed a habitual mental routine that lowered my level of happiness, I invested the time to go through each of the ABCDs.

At first, I found myself doing this exercise a dozen or more times each day. Then, only about 10 times a day, then 7 or 8, then 3 to 5. After only a month, it became habitual for my mind to skip from Adversity straight to Disputation without even picking up a pen.

Here's another example of how the ABCDs work. A man named Clay met a woman and invited her out to a local coffee shop. As they sipped tea and talked for several hours, it became obvious that they shared a strong, mutual attraction.

Clay promised to give her a call to arrange a date for later that week.

The following day, Clay called and got her voice mail. He left a message saying how enchanting he felt their time at the coffee shop had been. He said he would like to take her to dinner and a movie on Saturday. He said that he looked forward to a call back and left his number.

She didn't call back. The next day he called again. Still, no return call came.

Clay asked my advice and I suggested he go through this exercise. He went through steps A, B, and C easily, but when he got to D, he struggled. Sitting with his pen motionless, he seemed incapable of coming up with disputing beliefs.

"What if she lost her cell phone?" I prompted.

His look conveyed a mixture of irritation and uncertainty. "Aw, give me a break!" Clay said. "Now you're just making up excuses for her."

"Really?" I asked. "Have *you* ever lost *your* cell phone?"

He wrote down this disputation and several others.

The next time I saw him, Clay ran over to me. "She lost her cell phone!" he said. "That's why she didn't call me back. In fact, because she didn't have her phone, she was worried that I may not have called her."

"That's great," I said.

"Actually," he said, "the great part is that we had a date last Friday and it was wonderful!"

Taking the time to do this exercise will reveal both the cues that trigger you and your routine ways of thinking so that you can develop more positive ways of viewing events. Disputing your beliefs will create a positive feeling that will become your reward, solidifying this new mental process as a habit.

Look in the Rearview Mirror

Dick is a handsome, successful man who was still single well into his mid-forties. He sincerely wanted to get married and share his life with someone. Although he dated many beautiful and inter-esting women, none seemed to be "Miss Right."

One afternoon, Dick was driving along a highway, running late for a meeting, and not paying attention to how fast he was driving. A police officer pulled him over and wrote him a speeding ticket.

Putting his license back into his wallet, Dick mumbled angrily to himself. He put his car in drive and pulled back onto the highway. However, before he had traveled five more miles he was *again* pulled over and ticketed for speeding.

Two speeding tickets in 10 minutes—talk about a discouraging chain of events!

To avoid a significant increase in his insurance premiums, Dick opted to take a driver's training class offered by his state highway department. When he arrived at the class, Dick sat across from a beautiful brunette with brilliant green eyes. The two exchanged glances throughout the class.

After the class, the two went for coffee. They ultimately fell in love and married, and have been happy for several years.

Dick was triggered not once but *twice* by receiving speeding tickets. Although driving too fast was his own fault, he told me that he had felt angry and singled out for harassment by the police.

Dick had been searching for the woman of his dreams for several decades. He told me that if he had known that receiving those two tickets would have led to his meeting the love of his life, he would have driven even faster to make *certain* the cops stopped him.

Had he known then what he now knows, Dick's mental routine would have shifted. With the benefit of hindsight, he feels grateful for getting the tickets.

When I give a speech, I will often ask audience members to raise their hands if they are experiencing a particularly difficult problem. Typically, every hand will go up.

"Okay," I say. "Now raise your hand if you've ever had a difficult problem and it later turned out to be something that worked
out in your favor. For example, you lost your job and got a better
one as a result. Or a relationship ended and you then met someone who turned out to be the love of your life." Again, everyone
raises his or her hand.

"What if the problem you are now facing is actually in your
life as a catalyst to move you toward something better," I ask.
"What if you could shift your expectation about the difficulty
you are in so that you could believe that it is actually there to spin
your life off in a positive direction?"

I can see the wheels beginning to turn in their heads as they
consider this.

Our minds often play a trick on us. We almost always have
some sort of issue or problem we are facing, and in nearly every
case we not only get through the situation, we end up better off
for it.

However, our brains seem to have amnesia when it comes to
this process. "Sure, I made it through that problem I was having
a year ago," your brain says. "But this problem. . .*this problem* is
a big deal. This one is serious. I don't know that I can handle this
one, and even if I do, I don't think that there is any way something good will come as a result."

Life rarely makes sense looking through the front wind-
shield, but seeing how everything can align for your ultimate
benefit is possible when you view life through the rearview mirror. Projecting ourselves into the future, through a process called
"future journaling," allows us to develop new perspectives on
what once seemed to be challenging situations.

Laura King, a psychologist at the University of Missouri at Columbia, put future journaling to the test as a routine for raising happiness. As reported in *The How of Happiness* by Sonja Lyubomirsky, King had a group of students write a description of their best possible future selves for 20 minutes each day. After several weeks, the students reported an increase in their overall level of happiness.

When you are experiencing a down feeling or a problem situation, future journaling can shift your state quickly. Take out your journal and date the page six months or a year in the future. Next, begin to write out the way you want your life to be, as if it has already happened.

Be sure to write in full, vivid detail. Fill page after page of description so your subconscious mind can embrace the feelings of this idyllic future as a current reality.

Take whatever problem you are experiencing and write out how great your life will be when it is resolved. Here are some examples:

Situation	Ideal Future
You are having trouble connecting with your son.	"Today I spent a wonderful day talking with my son. He and I have really grown close and we enjoy..."
Your job is being eliminated.	"It's hard to believe I was worried when XYZ manufacturing let me go. My new job pays 20% more and I love what I'm doing. Why, just today I..."

You are diagnosed with a health challenge.	"It's only been six months since the doctor told me I was sick and at the time I was really worried, but I'm actually doing very well. In fact, I already. . ."
A relationship ends.	"I was so sad when she and I broke up. I thought I'd never get over it, and it did take several months for me to fully grieve. But it's been half a year and honestly, I feel great. I am feeling more at peace with who I am, and I. . ."

Life is going to trigger you repeatedly every single day. As you begin to practice new routines, they will become habitual. As the new habits replace old ones, you will find that maintaining a higher level of happiness becomes second nature.

REWARDS

The promise of dessert has inspired many a child to finish his or her vegetables. In fact, the certainty of dessert can make eating vegetables habitual.

Rewards are what turn routines into habits, because you begin to crave them. Craving rewards is what turns habits into perpetual motion machines.

The more you practice the thoughts, words, and actions from the three previous chapters, the happier you will begin to feel. Adding in the two routines from this chapter will also cause you to feel happier.

Happiness is, of course, reward enough. It is the reward we are seeking behind everything we want and everything we do. However, happiness is a gift that comes bearing other gifts.

Once you become a happier person, you find that your life improves in every way. When this begins to happen, you solidify your craving for happiness, and the activities and routines for happiness become as habitual as brushing your teeth.

Benefits of Cultivating a Higher Level of Happiness

To solidify a habit is to develop a craving for what you will receive once new routines have become habitual. The craving comes from experiencing, noticing, and appreciating the rewards.

Reading the list below of happiness rewards will help move you from focusing on happiness routines to craving the rewards of happiness. It will also make choosing happier thoughts, words, and actions a natural part of who you are when life triggers you.

I suggest you read this list often to remind you of what awaits you as you become a happier person.

A Longer Life

A National Academy of Sciences study found that people who are happy live, on average, 35% longer than their unhappy counterparts. Imagine—*35%*! This means that if people in your family tend to live to age 75, as a very happy person you could increase your life span to 101.

And in addition to an increased quantity of years, you will enjoy the immense quality of a happier life. A study published in the *Proceedings of the National Academy of Sciences* found that worry tends to diminish dramatically after age 50, meaning that you'd not only get more years but you'd also get more of the years that tend to be the happiest.

According to an article in London's *Daily Mail*, the reason older people are happier is that younger people tend to dwell on negative experiences until something positive distracts them, whereas older people tend to shrug off negative experiences.

Also studies have found that older people tend to cull from their friendships negative people who bring them down.

An Overall Increased Sense of Well-Being

Martin Seligman's research has shown that happy, optimistic people experience life differently. They tend to see positive events as:

- Personal
- Pervasive
- Permanent

That is, when something good happens, a happy person sees the fortunate event as proof of his or her value, an indication of other good things in that person's life, and something that will endure. Further, happy people see negative events as *not* being personal, pervasive, or permanent.

Greater Resilience in the Face of Challenges

A paper by Felicia A. Huppert from the University of Cambridge cites research stating that "positive emotions are associated with positive cognitive and social behaviour that may provide a basis for resilience throughout life."

Improved Health

A study published in the *Journal of Research in Personality* states, "Positive (happy) mood states play an important role in promoting physical health." Countless other studies have found that happiness increases levels of health-inducing blood chemicals that result in

- Less stress

- Lower blood pressure

- Fewer headaches

- Reduced body tension

- Less risk of diabetes

- Lower incidence of heart disease

A 2008 Gallup poll of people in 140 countries found that even in poorer nations where food, shelter, and water are limited, people who consider themselves to be happy report fewer physical ailments and illnesses.

Best-selling author and retired surgeon Bernie Siegel put it succinctly, "The simple truth is that happy people generally don't get sick."

And if that's not enough, here's the kicker! A study published by PreventDisease.com reported that becoming a happier person is even more beneficial to your health than quitting smoking.

You'll Become a Nicer Person

A study conducted by the Harvard Business School and the University of British Columbia found that kind people tend to be happy, and that happy people tend to be kind.

More Enjoyable and Enduring Relationships

For decades, researchers have reported that married people are happier than single people. However, new research shows that this finding is backward in its conclusion. It's *not* that married people are happier; rather, happy people tend to stay married!

Increased Self-Esteem

Several studies have found that a person's self-esteem is directly correlated to his or her level of happiness. The happier one is, the higher is his or her self-esteem.

More Money

As we discussed earlier, after a certain level of income is reached, money does not significantly affect happiness. However, a study by Michael Como titled "Do Happier People Make More Money?" published in *The Park Place Economist* found that high self-esteem is a key determinant in how much money one earns. Because happiness and self-esteem are directly proportionate, the higher a person's level of happiness, the more money he or she tends to earn.

More Free Time

A 30-year analysis conducted by Springer found that happy people spend less time watching television and being on the Internet. They spend more time connecting with others and pursuing their passions.

More Sex

The same Springer study reported that very happy people tend to have sex approximately 10 times more each year than do unhappy people. Incidentally, another study found that one of the fastest ways to feel happier is to have sex. So, being happy means more sex, and, having sex makes you feel happier.

Less Conflict and Discord

According to Med Jones in an article published by International Institute of Management, "Happy people are not concerned whether life is fair or not, they want to make the best of it."

Improved Brainpower

In the August 2, 2011, issue of *Psychology Today*, Susan Reynolds writes, "Happy people are more creative, solve problems faster, and tend to be more mentally alert."

Paying More Loving Attention to Others

Research shows that unhappy people spend a great deal of time ruminating about themselves and their lives. Happy people are less caught up in themselves and can focus more attention on others.

Improved Performance at Work

In a 2010 study, James K. Harter and his associates found a distinct correlation between happiness and performance at work. A study by Martin Seligman of 272 workers over an 18-month period showed that happier people receive better job evaluations and higher pay. The happier you are, the more you get done and the greater your satisfaction and rewards.

Old Habits Never Die

Be aware that researchers have discovered another aspect to habits that is important to remember with regard to happiness.

Studies have found that old habits never go away. Rats that habitually ran through a maze a certain way when cued will run the same course again when a similar cue is issued—even when they know that the reward they seek has been moved and can only be found by taking a different path. Old habits diminish, but the cue > routine of old habits *never* fades completely even when the reward goes away.

After having given up smoking for more than two decades, I accepted a cigarette offered by a friend and soon found that I was back to smoking every day. The smoking habit had never left me; it had only retreated into the shadows of my psyche.

I did find, however, that quitting smoking the second time was easier than before, because I had developed new routines and rewards that I could call upon when triggered to grab a cigarette.

It has often been said that "the price of freedom is eternal vigilance." To be a happy person in a world that tends to celebrate cynicism, sarcasm, complacency, fear, and victimhood requires constant vigilance. You need to remember to practice happiness routines when triggered by life for your higher level of happiness to endure.

Just as a person who faithfully exercises and carefully selects the foods that will nourish his or her body will, over time, lose the new level of fitness if these practices are not maintained, so too will a person who develops the habits of living a happier life fall back to a lower happiness level if supporting thoughts, words, and actions are not rigorously maintained.

If your happiness stone rolls down the hill, you will find that, unlike Sisyphus, you are becoming stronger and better able to push it back up more quickly and maintain it longer.

You will have new happiness habits that can override previous unhappiness habits.

And because you have begun to crave the dozens of benefits of being a happier person, you will gravitate to happiness habits more easily and be able to maintain them for longer periods. In short, choosing happiness habits will become, well, habitual!

The Pursuit of Happiness

English poet Alexander Pope wrote, "Oh happiness! our being's end and aim!"

Why? Because without happiness nothing else matters. When you are happy, everything else gets better. Happiness is the reward that we seek for everything we do. And being happy brings rewards to every area of our lives.

The United States' Declaration of Independence states, "We hold these truths to be self-evident, that all men are created equal, that they are endowed by their Creator with certain unalienable Rights, that among these are Life, Liberty and the pursuit of Happiness."

To our colonial forefathers, the word "pursuit" did not mean "to pursue" or "to go after." Rather, it meant "something one practices," such as a person might engage in the pursuit or practice of being a doctor, lawyer, businessman, or student.

Happiness is a pursuit. It is a mode of being. Happiness is a habitual way of living.

In *The Power of Positive Thinking*, Norman Vincent Peale wrote, "Our happiness depends on the habit of mind we cultivate. So practice happy thinking every day. Cultivate the merry heart, develop the happiness habit, and life will become a continual feast."

RECAPPING "HABITS OF HAPPINESS"

- Notice what cues cause a decrease in your level of happiness, and begin to develop new triggers.

- Consider how you might have felt rewarded in the past from having a low happiness level. Notice when you habitually respond to cues with routines that take your mood down, and resolve to practice new routines that keep your happiness level high.

- Whenever something cues you causing you to feel unhappy, practice your ABCDs. Do this every time you feel a negative emotional reaction until it becomes automatic.

- Create a clear vision of your happier life by investing 20 minutes daily in future journaling.

- Develop a craving for happiness. A couple of times each day, read the list of rewards that come as side benefits of cultivating a higher level of happiness.

CHAPTER SEVEN

Character of Happiness

The just man is happy, and the unjust man is miserable.
—Plato

He stood on a mountaintop six hundred feet above the valley below. He was shirtless, wearing jeans, a cowboy hat, and boots. He squinted into the bright, clear blue sky as with one calloused hand he gripped the heavy hammer and with the other placed the blade of his long chisel on the surface of the granite beneath his feet.

Raising the hammer skyward, he drew in a deep breath. He exhaled as he brought the hammer down with all the force he could muster. The hammer met its mark, and a shrill *click* echoed down the mountainside. The reverberation caused an elk to freeze momentarily and a hawk to take flight from its perch. That first hammer strike would send a shock wave that would touch millions of lives for all time.

Carving a Mountain

The year was 1948, and the man's name was Korczak Ziolkowski (pronounced *CORE-chalk jewel-CUFF-ski*), a Polish immigrant to the United States. Although he had never received any formal art training, he was embarking on the creation of the largest and most ambitious sculpture in human history. Whereas everyone else saw only the craggy Black Hills, Korczak saw a monument to the spirit of one of the most legendary figures in US history.

He had come to the mountain alone to undertake this mammoth and historic task. A task many considered to be impossible. He was 40 years old the day he climbed that mountain near the Badlands of South Dakota, hammer and chisel in hand. He would spend the rest of his life on that mountain, braving both the summer heat and the vicious South Dakota winters, until he died at age 74.

Orphaned at age 1, Korczak had bounced around various foster homes. In his teens, he was apprenticed to a shipbuilder as a wood-carver. By 20, he had become an accomplished furniture maker. At 31, Korczak served briefly as assistant to Gutzon Borglum in the sculpting of Mount Rushmore.

Korczak's breathtakingly lifelike sculpture of the Polish composer and political leader Ignacy Jan Paderewski earned him fame when it won first prize at the 1939 New York World's Fair. Korczak might have opted for a life of ease sculpting the rich and famous, but he made a very different choice instead.

Henry Standing Bear, chief of the Ponca Tribe—a willowy man with a hawk's-beak nose and intense but friendly eyes—contacted Korczak on behalf of several Native American elders asking if he would carve a memorial to the Sioux chief Crazy Horse out of one of the peaks in South Dakota's Black Hills. Chief Henry Standing Bear said, "My fellow chiefs and I would like the white man to know the red man has great heroes, too."

Korczak and Chief Henry Standing Bear selected Thunderhead Mountain near Custer, South Dakota, as the site for the memorial. Although the mountain was not chosen for its name, the name Thunderhead is significant to the story of the great Crazy Horse.

Thunder Dreamers

Back when I visited Heyoka Reed Brown's home on the Pine Ridge Reservation, we sat one morning listening to the local radio station as it played the lilting chants and rhythmic drums of Native American performers. One of the ancient songs faded, and in a jarring segue the song "Thunderstruck" by AC/DC came on. I silently wondered if somehow the radio signal had drifted.

Reed saw my bewildered expression, and the smile on his face told me that this music selection was neither incongruous nor accidental. "According to Lakota tradition," he said, "a person who has a dream of thunder is being called to a high purpose."

He paused a moment as Brian Johnson, AC/DC's lead singer, growled the lyrics. Reed gave me a playful smile and said softly, "Thunder dreamers are also known by another name: Heyoka."

The World's Most Famous Sacred Clown

In the mid-1850s, a teenage Lakota boy named Cha-O-Ha slept and had a vivid dream of thunder. This was a blessed watershed moment in his life. This dream called him to become a Heyoka and he began to be mentored by an elder of his tribe in the sacred ways of this esteemed position.

Cha-O-Ha (or "Light Hair," as his mother called him) distinguished himself in battle, and as a reward for his bravery his father gave his own name over to Cha-O-Ha. The father's name had been "His Horse Must Be Crazy." White settlers would later interpret the young brave's name as "Crazy Horse."

Crazy Horse was a thunder dreamer, a Heyoka, a Sacred Clown. It is therefore an expression of universal karma that Thunderhead Mountain was selected for the monument to his spirit.

From $174 to 741 Steps

Prior to beginning work, Korczak spent seven years studying Native American history. He arrived in South Dakota with only $174 in his pocket. He lived in a tent and bought land nearby upon which he built a log home.

Having created reasonable shelter for himself, Korczak cut down trees to build a stairway towering 741 steps up the side of Thunderhead Mountain. Every day, he trudged up the steps, carrying hundreds of pounds of equipment.

When finished, the memorial would be a massive 563 feet high and 641 feet wide.

To fully comprehend how big the Crazy Horse Memorial really is, you need to know that the entirety of the Mount Rushmore sculpture would fit easily inside the carving of just Crazy Horse's head. Crazy Horse's memorial would ultimately display not only his head but also the great chief's upper torso, arms, and even the front third of his horse.

Unlike the statues of George Washington, Thomas Jefferson, Theodore Roosevelt, and Abraham Lincoln carved into Mount Rushmore, the Crazy Horse Memorial was designed by Korczak to be in the round. That is, whereas on Mount Rushmore you see only the front of the presidents' faces, the Crazy Horse memorial would depict the great chief from all sides: a 360-degree view.

With his design approved, Korczak set to work. He chiseled holes in the ground, in which he placed dynamite to blast away extraneous earth and rock.

The hours were long and the work physically demanding. Very early on, Korczak fell and injured himself. He later broke both his wrist and his thumb. One day he slipped while working and tore his Achilles tendon. And yet he worked on.

From the crushing weight of the tools he carried up and down the mountain each day, Korczak had to have two major back surgeries that removed a total of three spinal disks. He once had an accident wherein he lost control of an earthmover and drove it over the side of the mountain; he fell dozens of feet. Korczak was back at work with a cast on his leg driving the same earthmover the very next day. He suffered two heart attacks, one of them severe, and yet he never stopped. His vision was a tidal wave that pulled him along and swept up tens of thousands of others in its wake.

A Self-Portrait of Happiness

As I toured the welcome center—where off in the distance you can see the work begun by Korczak being continued by 7 of his 10 children—I saw many of Korczak's sculptures and paintings. The one that struck me the most was a self-portrait Korczak had painted of himself and his beloved wife, Ruth.

In the painting, the two of them are smiling broadly; they seem on the verge of breaking into joyous laughter. The happiness in their faces radiates from the canvas. It is a brilliant depiction of two people who are obviously very happy.

In Chapter 5, I shared studies reporting that the wider a person smiled in his or her yearbook or Facebook photo, the happier that person tended to be later in life. Korczak saw himself and his love as being extremely happy, and the photograph of the two of them that adorns the back cover of the photographic history book of the Crazy Horse Memorial shows that same joie de vivre as they lived the twilight of their lives.

Korczak was a man engrossed in a life's work that filled him with a daily sense of purpose—even though he knew that what he had begun would never be completed during his lifetime. In 1998, fifty years to the day after the mountain was dedicated and sixteen years after Korczak's death, the carved face of Crazy Horse was publicly unveiled for the first time. Prior to that ceremony, nothing remotely resembling a sculpture had been evident.

Crazy Horse himself said, "A very great vision is needed, and the man who has it must follow it as the eagle seeks the deepest blue of the sky." Certainly, Korczak had such a vision and followed it. Yet beyond being a man of great vision, Korczak was a man of great character.

Character Defined

One way for "character" to be defined is as follows: "one of the attributes or features that make up and distinguish the individual." Korczak's passion for his work was certainly a distinguishing part of who he was and, no doubt, led to his happily facing a literal mountain of work each day.

Another definition of "character" is "moral or ethical quality."

Here, too, Korczak was a man of character. As word of the memorial spread and donations began to pour in, he could have easily justified paying himself a generous salary as designer, foreman, and chief worker on the project. But Korczak never once accepted payment for his work on the Crazy Horse Memorial. The more money the nonprofit Crazy Horse Memorial Foundation had, the more machinery and supplies could be purchased, and

Korczak did not want to siphon resources away from this important endeavor.

Korczak saw the memorial as more than just a mountain carving. In addition to the gigantic sculpture that, when completed, will tower approximately one-half the height of the now demolished World Trade Center towers in New York City, Korczak planned for the site to be home for the Indian Museum of North America, the Native American Cultural Center, and the Indian University of North America.

Such a vision takes resources, and there were times when money was sorely needed. However, Korczak twice turned down offers of $10 million from the US government. He felt that he could not with integrity accept money from the government that had nearly driven Native Americans to the brink of extinction.

High ideals capture the imagination of people and engage the power of the universe. Korczak was too busy pursuing his dream to study the connection between character and happiness, but if he had, he would have found that character and happiness have been intrinsically intertwined throughout humankind's existence.

The Ubiquitous Golden Rule

Treating others with kindness and fairness positively correlates to happiness. A person who lives life by the Golden Rule is far more likely to be happy.

In our culture when we read the term "the Golden Rule," we tend to associate it with Jesus's comment found in both the books of Matthew and Luke in the Christian Bible. However, the idea of treating others as we ourselves would like to be treated is one of the most ubiquitous ideals expressed in all theologies and philosophies. Consider:

Christianity

*Do unto others as you would
have them do unto you.*
—Matthew 7:12 and
Luke 6:31

Islam

*No one of you is a be-
liever until he desires for
his brother that which
he desires for himself.*
—Hadith recorded by
al-Bukhari, Sunnah

Judaism

Love your neighbor as yourself.
—Leviticus 19:18

Hinduism

*This is the sum of duty;
do naught onto others
that you would not have
them do unto you.*
—Mahabharata 5:1517

Buddhism

*Hurt not others in ways that you
yourself would find hurtful.*
—Udanavarga 5:18

Taoism

*Regard your neighbor's gain
as your gain, and your neighbor's loss as your own loss.*
—T'ai-shang Kan-ying P'ien

Confucianism

*Do not do to others what you
would not like yourself.*
—Analects 12:2

Zoroastrianism

*Whatever is disagree-
able to yourself
do not do unto others.*
—Shayast-na-Shayast 13

Baha'i

*He should not wish for others what
he does not wish for himself.*
—Bahá' Alláh, Baha'i Faith

Humanism

*Don't do things you
wouldn't want
to have done to you.*
—British Humanist
Association

Wicca

*Bide the Wiccan Rede ye must,
In Perfect Love and Perfect
Trust. Live ye must and let to
live, Fairly take and fairly give.*
—THE WICCAN REDE OPEN-
ING STATEMENT

Sufism

*The basis of Sufism is
consideration of
the hearts and feelings of others.*
—JAVAD NURBAKHSH, MASTER OF
THE NIMATULLAHI SUFI ORDER

Scientology

*Try to treat others as you would
want them to treat you.*
—L. RON HUBBARD, THE
WAY TO HAPPINESS

Brahmanism

*This is the sum of Dharma
[duty]: Do naught unto others which would cause you
pain if done to you.*
—MAHABHARATA, 5:1517

Native American Spirituality

*Do not wrong or hate
your neighbor.
For it is not he who you
wrong, but yourself.*
—PIMA PROVERB

Ancient Egyptian

*Do for one who may
do for you,
That you may cause
him thus to do.*
—THE TALE OF THE ELOQUENT
PEASANT 109–110, TRANS-
LATED BY R. B. PARKINSON

Ancient Greek

*Do not do to others that
which would anger you
if others did it to you.*
—ISOCRATES

Jainism

*Therefore, neither does he
cause violence to others nor
does he make others do so.*
—ACARANGA SUTRA 5:101-2

The purpose of religion and spirituality is to lead people to a happier state of being either in this life or, as some people and cultures believe, in the next.

The Golden Rule's suggestion that we should treat other people as we ourselves would like to be treated is not a moral injunction. Rather, it is a statement of a universally understood principle that leads to happiness.

What we do to others, we do to ourselves, because we are all of the same spirit. When we harm another person, we harm ourselves. We cannot do harm to others—which would lead to their being less happy—and be genuinely happy ourselves.

People Can Only Do What They Believe to Be Right

"Wait a minute," you may be thinking. "I could name dozens of examples where people have treated other people badly and it has not affected their happiness."

Actually, no you can't. In fact, I'll go one step further and state that human beings cannot be happy doing that which they *know* to be wrong.

For a person to do something wrong, that person must feel that his or her actions are justified. When we justify something, we are attempting to bring justice to a situation—the unstated belief is that there already exists an injustice. Therefore, an act that might be considered immoral or wrong is often done in the unspoken and unrealized belief that it will bring balance where there is a perceived moral imbalance.

Certainly there are people who suffer from mental disorders who are incapable of telling right from wrong. However, mentally healthy people cannot do what they know to be wrong without justifying their actions. If you've ever read Dostoyevsky's *Crime and Punishment*, you know the story of the main character, Raskolnikov, who commits murder, and his soul and psyche burn with the knowledge of his deed for the rest of his life.

A person who knowingly harms another person cannot be happy. The Buddhist leader Daisaku Ikeda has said, "It is impossible to build one's own happiness on the unhappiness of others."

People who do harm to others must justify their actions to themselves, and in some cases to other people, by rationalizing their behavior. They tell themselves "rational lies" to justify what they have done. In so doing, they lower their levels of happiness.

A Teaching Moment Leads to Happiness

Ten years ago, when my daughter, Lia, was six, we were visiting my brother in Columbia, South Carolina. We were with him for several days, and one night she and I went out to purchase some groceries. We drove 15 minutes to the grocery store, parked, and went inside to do our shopping.

We then got back into our car and drove the 15-minute trip back to my brother's home. As we unpacked the groceries, I found a box of toothpicks in one of the grocery bags. Toothpicks had not been on our shopping list and I couldn't remember purchasing them. I pulled out the store receipt and checked to see if we had been charged for the toothpicks. We had not.

The box of toothpicks retailed for 65¢. At that moment, I had a choice. I could simply keep the toothpicks or I could make the half-hour round-trip back to the store, spending more in gas than the cost of the toothpicks.

I saw this as an opportunity to teach Lia the importance of honesty, and so she and I got back into the car and drove to the store. I held her small hand as we carried the box of toothpicks to one of the registers.

I explained to the young cashier that we had gotten home and discovered that the toothpicks were in our bag and that I wanted to return them because we had not paid for them. The woman was obviously surprised that I had gone to so much trouble over such an insignificant item, but thanked me and took them.

As we drove back to my brother's home, I realized that I felt happy. I wondered if this was because I had demonstrated the importance of doing the right thing to my impressionable daughter. As I delved more deeply into my happy feeling, I realized that it was not the result of teaching my daughter a lesson. Rather, I was simply happier because I had done the right thing.

The Link Between Ethics and Happiness
Harvey James, an economics professor at the University of Missouri at Columbia, has been studying the link between ethical behavior and happiness.

It all began when he read the 2005–2006 *World Values Survey*, which attempts to measure attitudes of people around the world. Respondents were interviewed and asked to state how satisfied they were with their lives on a scale from 1 to 10. (Does this sound familiar?)

Additionally, respondents were asked four ethical questions:

1. How acceptable do you consider it be to claim government benefits to which you are not entitled?
2. How acceptable do you consider it be to avoid paying your fare on public transportation?
3. How acceptable do you consider it be to cheat on your taxes?
4. How acceptable do you consider it be to accept a bribe?

When James crunched the numbers, he found that "people who believe that these particular ethical scenarios are not acceptable also tend to indicate they are more satisfied with life. That's with controlling for other factors that scholars have shown are also correlated with happiness, including relative wealth."

James told me, "The more likely people are to state that it's very inappropriate to engage in unethical acts, the more likely they are to report higher levels of happiness."

James and I discussed the concept of gross national happiness (GNH) versus gross national product (GNP) as the primary indicator of a country's vitality. James, who you'll remember is an economist and should be inclined to support economic factors, instead stated that GNH is the most important measurement.

"Why?" I asked.

"Because a robust economy does not increase happiness," he answered. "But, happiness could be one of the greatest catalysts for boosting a country's economic growth."

And one of the most important contributors to happiness, James believes, is ethics.

"If a country's goal is to improve subjective well-being, and if subjective well-being increases when people are ethical," he explained, "then efforts to improve the moral behavior of people will also improve overall societal well-being and prosperity."

"The challenge," he told me, "is that governments put their focus on laws. Laws don't inspire ethical behavior, they inspire compliance, and people follow laws only to the degree that they fear they might get caught."

Laws are external and therefore cannot impact happiness. You cannot legislate morality. You cannot create laws that will force people to adopt ethical behavior. Every year, three hundred new laws are passed in the United States, and this has been the case since the 1970s. That means that, in the last four decades, a staggering 12,000 new laws have been passed.

Certainly, many categories of crime are down in the United States over the last half century, but the crimes that have diminished—such as murder, rape, and violent assault—were already on the books. Government officials seem incapable of inspiring people to adopt ethical behavior and so they constantly enact new laws because they don't know what else to do. Besides, new laws attract media attention and increase political clout.

We all know the concept of motivating behavior utilizing either "the carrot" or "the stick." This idiomatic expression goes back to farmers who either dangled a carrot in front of a mule, enticing the mule to move forward, or whipped the mule with a stick, to drive it forward.

"It seems to me that government only knows about administering the stick through laws and punishment for infractions," I said to James.

"Right," he said. "What we need is a carrot to get people to *want* to act more ethically, and that carrot is increased happiness."

As we discussed in the previous chapter, it is the craving for a reward that gets us to make a routine habitual. The *absence* of something cannot motivate you. You don't develop a craving for *not* getting a traffic ticket or *not* being audited, therefore there is little incentive other than the fear of punishment for being caught. This does not lead to ethical behavior but self-protective behavior, which is not correlated with happiness.

James said that countries could begin to promote feeling happier as the reward for treating others well and, in the end, end up with fewer lawsuits, a happier populace, *and* a more vital economy.

Countries that are attempting to increase their GNP rating would be well advised to consider intrinsic motivators in addition to extrinsic ones. Decent wages, safety, and access to health care are important. However, a country where people feel that they can trust their government to do what it says it will do and to treat individuals in a fair and evenhanded manner creates an atmosphere for greater happiness among its citizenry.

"There is a lot of research that shows that countries that respect the rights of the individual tend to have happier people," James told me. "There is evidence that shows that countries where there is a great deal of trust tend to have both happier citizens *and* higher economic growth."

Many people act unethically and rationalize away their behavior, telling themselves that others are already unethical and so they are just trying to protect themselves and level the playing field. They concede that the Golden Rule may instruct us to "do unto others as we would have them do unto us," but they believe that because others are already doing them wrong, their unethical behavior is a reasonable reaction.

To adopt such as position is to set yourself up as a victim and to excuse your own shady dealings as a validated response to what you perceive others to be doing.

The Golden Rule makes no reference to how other people act. It doesn't say, "Treat anyone badly who first treats you badly." The Golden Rule is not concerned with another person's actions at all.

Early twentieth-century American theologian and columnist Frank Crane wrote, "The Golden Rule is of no use to you whatsoever unless you realize that it's your move." It is up to each of us to act in an ethical manner because doing so will make *us* happier. Rather than waiting for others to shine the light of ethics into society, most people shrug their shoulders at the darkness of unethical behavior, all the while dwelling in misery in that very darkness.

It's Better to Light a Single Candle than to Curse the Darkness

In the mid-1700s, Benjamin Franklin ran a newspaper in Philadelphia. In reviewing the stories he published on robbery and violent crime, Franklin noticed that most of these crimes occurred at night on the city's darkened streets. He realized that rarely, if ever, was a criminal bold enough to rob or attack someone in broad daylight.

In an effort to make his beloved city safer, Franklin petitioned the city of Philadelphia to install gas streetlamps along the city's busiest streets. The city declined. At that time, it was not the norm for cities to provide street lighting.

Franklin then approached local merchants asking them to install streetlamps in front of their businesses. Each refused, stating that such an expense could not be justified.

The darkness of colonial Philadelphia streets is like the unethical behavior that permeates many societies. It has the potential to negatively impact everyone. Asking others to change the situation rarely does any good, because people tend to follow along with the way other people do things. In advertising, this is known as the "bandwagon effect." People feel justified in their actions or inactions so long as they are riding along on the same bandwagon as others.

For change to occur, someone must be willing to step off the bandwagon.

Franklin was only one person in a city of more than thirty thousand. He had asked others to bring light into their collective darkness, but they had refused. Franklin would have been justified in giving up. But he didn't.

An ancient Chinese proverb states, "It is better to light a single candle than to curse the darkness," and this is exactly what Franklin did. Franklin invested his own money to install a single streetlamp in front of his newspaper office.

At first, few people noticed or commented on Franklin's streetlamp. Soon, however, shopkeepers began to observe people congregating in the evening beneath the streetlamp in front of Franklin's business. They witnessed women hurrying past the darkness in front of their stores to the safety of the light coming from Franklin's lone streetlamp.

Soon, another business owner invested in a streetlamp and began to attract evening customers. To his surprise, that shopkeeper noticed that his daytime business also increased due to the goodwill engendered from his having provided a little more safety and security to the citizens of Philadelphia.

Another shopkeeper followed suit, then another, and another. In time, streetlamps were no longer considered an optional luxury but instead seen as a community necessity; their installation and maintenance were taken over by the city.

And, as Franklin had hoped would happen, he had fewer crimes to report in his newspaper.

Benjamin Franklin brought a single light into the darkness of Philadelphia and, as a result, he got to live in a safer city. Franklin could have wrung his hands and complained that "someone should do something," but he realized that someone is almost always ourselves.

You are a drop in the ocean that is your society. As you act with greater integrity, you raise the overall purity of the waters. Other people will follow suit and you will get to enjoy living in the safety of a more trustworthy society, which research has found to be a key contributor to happiness.

Just as Franklin could not have predicted which shopkeeper would be the first to follow his lead and install a streetlamp, you cannot say for certain who will follow your stance of character; but you can be assured it will happen. As people see that you are dealing fairly with them and that you place their welfare on par with your own, you will see the light beginning to spread when they, in turn, act this way toward others.

With happiness as your goal, it is incumbent upon you to evaluate how you are doing in the fair-dealing department and to begin to shift toward being as ethical as you possibly can be.

You don't do this to appease others or even God. You do this simply because the reward for treating others well is your own happiness. The more ethically you treat other people, the happier you begin to feel. Soon, you will begin to crave the increased level of happiness, and acting in ethical ways will become a routine habit.

On the subject of God, some expressions of religion are not unlike Congress and state legislatures. Rather than encouraging people to be moral so that they will reap the reward of inner peace and happiness, some religions demand that people act morally or run the risk of eternal damnation.

The word "religion" literally means "to bind together," and some people take this literally, binding their teachings together into a stick to whack people. A person running afoul of religious rules is threatened with hellfire or, at the very least, guilt. This practice instills a sense of fear and shame, and you cannot be happy if you feel afraid or ashamed.

We often hear of people who are strident in their religious teachings "falling from grace" and acting immorally. This is because focusing on punishment rather than reward makes people unhappy and a person who is unhappy is *less likely* to act in a morally upright fashion. Rather than threatening their followers, religious leaders would do well to teach people of the joy that comes from having a clean conscience and the happiness that follows as a natural result. They should emphasize the carrot and not the stick.

Treat Everyone like Beloved Family

The teachings of Confucius are the moral underpinning of China. The essence of Confucius's philosophy is to treat everyone as if he or she were a member of one's own family. Unfortunately, many people treat others differently from members of their family. It might be unconscionable to take unfair advantage of a member of one's own family, but they think members of other people's families are fair game.

The moment we draw a circle around our family and ourselves, and place others on the outside of that circle, we separate from the most basic of spiritual truths: we are all one family. We fragment our spiritual wholeness, and in our fragmentation we diminish our own happiness.

In addition to treating others fairly, honesty is another important aspect of character. And, not surprisingly, correlations between telling the truth and happiness have been documented.

Honesty Is Not Only the Best Policy— It's a Direct Route to Happiness

Researchers at the University of Notre Dame recruited 110 individuals between the ages of 18 and 71 to participate in a 10-week experiment. They divided the subjects into two groups.

The first group was instructed to avoid lying. If confronted with a situation where telling the truth made them uncomfortable, they were advised to simply remain silent if possible. But, regardless of what transpired, they were to do their best not to lie during the course of the experiment.

The other group was a control group and was given no special instructions regarding being honest.

Each week, everyone in both groups came in to receive health and relationship evaluations, as well as polygraphs to assess how often they had lied during the previous week.

The results were impressive and significant. The group that was asked to forgo telling lies reported fewer mental health issues, such as anxiety and sadness, as well as fewer physical ailments, such as headaches and sore throats. In addition, the group that was instructed to not lie during the 10-week experiment reported improvements in their close personal relationships.

It's ironic that people often fear that telling the truth might damage their relationships, because this research shows exactly the opposite. The more honest people are, the closer their relationships.

The study found that honest people experienced less anxiety and sadness. To have less sadness is to have more happiness. But, why would honesty be positively correlated with happiness?

Lying Limits Happiness

Awhile back I was with a group of friends and we were talking about honesty. One of them said something truly profound: "Fear precedes every lie ever told." I thought about his comment for quite some time and I realized it is true.

People lie because they are afraid. People lie because they are afraid that they will be blamed for something. People lie because they are afraid of having to have an uncomfortable conversation.

People lie because they are afraid that telling the truth might make them unsafe.

A lie is a result of fear, and you can't simultaneously be afraid and be happy.

Embellishing the truth is lying. People embellish the truth to exaggerate their own importance, because they are afraid that by telling the truth they might be judged as being insufficient.

For example, a high school basketball player might score 11 points during a game, but later tell his grandparents that he made 17 points because he knows that one of his cousins tends to average about 17 points per game. He is afraid of being compared unfavorably to his cousin and so he exaggerates the truth of his performance.

When a person embellishes his or her performance, it is with the intention of lessening fear in hopes of raising his or her happiness level. However, because an embellishment is a lie, it has the opposite effect and leads to unhappiness, because the person knows that what he or she said is not genuine.

Lying to exaggerate one's importance is another way of saying, "Let me tell you I'm better than I am because I'm afraid that I'm not good enough." Unfortunately, the internal belief of "I'm not good enough" is an indicator of his or her low self-esteem and, as we've already discussed, self-esteem and happiness are proportionate.

Liberation through a Piracy Purge

About a decade ago, I was experiencing a profound feeling of inadequacy. I was struggling financially and not feeling very happy. At the time, I thought my unhappiness was a result of not having much money, but I see now that my unhappiness had more to do with my feeling of inadequacy than my bank balance.

One afternoon, I went into my office to listen to some music. As I dug through my CDs, I noticed something. Several of the CDs were pirated copies that had been burned for me by other people.

On a hunch, I walked into our living room and opened the drawer containing our collection of videotapes. There I saw nearly a dozen pirated tapes that I had copied or which had been given to me by friends or family members. I next checked my computer and realized that I had several software programs that were illegal copies obtained from friends and colleagues.

I called a family meeting.

"If we had ten million dollars in the bank," I said, "would we still be stealing music, movies, and software by having illegal copies?"

"We didn't steal them," my daughter said. "People gave them to us."

"Did we pay for them?" I asked.

All heads shook. "No."

"So," I said, "even if we didn't steal them, we are in possession of stolen goods. Would we do that if we had millions of dollars at our disposal?"

My family stared back at me for a long moment and then said, one by one, "Well, no, I guess not."

"Then we need to stop living like we're poor thieves and begin to act as wealthy people of integrity, and we need to do it now—not wait until we have a lot of money," I said. "I want each of you to dig through your CDs and tapes and pull out anything we didn't pay for, because we're going to get rid of it all."

They looked at me in disbelief for a long moment but then left the room to do as I asked. Ten minutes later, we all met outside in front of the barrel we used to burn our trash.

"Let's get rid of this stuff now," I said. "The people who created these products deserve compensation for their work, and just because 'everyone else does it,' it doesn't justify our acting out of integrity."

I lit a fire and we began to drop the items in one by one. We then went back into the house and deleted all the pirated software from our two computers. We didn't do any of this out of a fear of being caught. Rather, we did it because we chose to be in alignment with what was ethical.

"They must often change, who would be constant in happiness or wisdom," said Confucius—and purging ourselves of pirated media was a big change for us. However, this stands out in my mind as one of the defining moments in both my level of happiness and our level of prosperity.

To this day, I will not accept pirated software or movies. If someone gives me a CD that is a burned copy, I will go onto iTunes and pay for the CD even if I don't download it. I have a copy, so I pay for it.

People sometimes look askance at me for being so diligent in my character. I have even had people attack me for being this way because they feel that I must, somehow, be judging them for what they choose to do.

I don't judge them. What they choose to do or not do is of no concern to me whatsoever. I simply place a high value on my own happiness, and I know that happiness and character go hand in hand.

Becoming Super Human

Aristotle declared, "Happiness is the meaning and the purpose of life, the whole aim and end of human existence." Aristotle would have used the word *eudaimonia*, the Greek word commonly translated as "happiness." Etymologically, it is comprised of *eu* (good) and *daimōn* (a type of supernatural being).

Most people justify a lack of character as simply being on the bandwagon with everyone else. "It's only human," they say. "It's just natural."

The level of happiness we are aspiring to reach is not "only human." Rather, it is eudaemonic, "good to the point of being supernatural."

Eudaemonia is a central point in Aristotle's writings. To Aristotle, happiness and ethics were indelibly intertwined. He wrote, "Happiness is the highest good, being a realization and perfect practice of virtue."

An unethical person may drink from the momentary and shallow well of attainment, but he or she will never know the deep and lasting oasis of happiness.

Happy people are people of character not because a government or religious authority says that they must be ethical; they are this way because it brings them happiness.

Ayn Rand, the brilliant author of *Atlas Shrugged*, succinctly put it: "My philosophy in essence is the concept of man as a heroic being with his own happiness as the moral purpose of this life."

As people raise their happiness level, their character naturally rises. And, as people act with character, their happiness levels increase proportionately.

RECAPPING "CHARACTER OF HAPPINESS"

- You can't be out of integrity and truly be happy, because you will have subtle feelings of fear that you will be caught or that others will cheat you—both of which negate happiness.

- Afford everyone you come in contact with the same fair treatment you would extend to a beloved family member.

- Cease to excuse your shady dealings with "rational lies."

- Speak the truth at all times or remain silent.

- Don't embellish your accomplishments; when you do, your attempts to inflate your importance in the eyes of others diminishes your self-importance, which lowers your level of happiness.

CHAPTER EIGHT

Destiny of Happiness

Destiny is not a matter of chance; it is a matter of choice. It is not a thing to be waited for; it is a thing to be achieved.
—William Jennings Bryan

"Rats!" I muttered as I watched the interstate traffic ahead come to a stop for the fourth time that half hour. Between stops, the speed of our car had barely gotten above 15 miles per hour. "Change lanes," I suggested.

"The other lane isn't moving either," my friend said.

"We're going to be late," I repeated for perhaps the tenth time.

"It can't be helped," she said. "This is the only way to get there, and they are paving the highway." Then she added, "You're just going to have to let it go."

The "it" she was suggesting I "let go" was the chance to meet a celebrity I had admired for many years.

Yakov Smirnoff, the bearded little man with a sharp wit and a warm smile, was one of my favorite comedians. During the height of the Cold War between the United States and the Soviet Union, Yakov had immigrated to the United States. He spent several years playing comedy clubs, offering witty observations comparing customs and conditions in the United States with those of his native Russia.

After the Cold War ended and the Russians became US allies, Yakov moved to Branson, Missouri, opening what would become one of the largest and most successful theaters in that tourist mecca. A few years later, Yakov was presenting a condensed version of his hit Broadway show *Happily Ever Laughter* in Springfield, Missouri, which I hoped to see. Better yet, I had a friend who was the coordinator of the event, and she promised that if I arrived early, she would make certain I would meet Yakov.

I had been on an emotional high all week and found myself repeating over and over to myself, "I'm going to meet Yakov. I'm going to meet Yakov." All of this should help put in perspective why my friends and I were enduring this three-and-a-half-hour drive in stop-and-go traffic and why I was so stressed out at the time. Suddenly, the prospect of meeting Yakov seemed out of the question.

As our car finally turned off the highway onto the exit that led to the venue, I looked at the clock realizing we'd be lucky to even get there before the show began. My shoulders slumped and I let out a long sigh. As we drove closer to the venue, I realized that traffic was, again, coming to a halt.

"Now what?" I asked, craning my head to see what was going on up ahead.

It just so happened that there was a major classic car show in Springfield that very weekend. Police had stopped traffic to allow the hundred-plus cars to pull out. A long parade of refurbished vehicles snaked ahead of us.

Inside I felt hopeless, but I knew the power of sticking to an intention. "I'm going to meet Yakov," I said in my mind. "I'm going to meet Yakov."

Twenty minutes later, the traffic crept forward. Although we were running late, I continued to affirm "I'm going to meet Yakov."

Jarring me back to reality, my friend suddenly asked, "What's that?"

"Where?" I said.

"There," she said, pointing to spot a few hundred feet ahead.

Focusing my gaze in the direction she was pointing, I could see cars swerving slowly around something that blocked the road. Small puffs of dirt cascaded in the air.

As we drew closer, I saw a barefoot and bare-chested young boy in tattered shorts standing in the middle of traffic, playfully throwing handfuls of dirt into the air. One by one, cars veered around him, but no one stopped.

I scanned the side of the street, looking for an adult who might have accidentally allowed the youngster to slip away, but I saw no one. Here, in the middle of a busy six-lane street was a young child, oblivious to the danger of the moving cars all around him. He was simply making a game of reaching down and grabbing handfuls of dirt that lay on the road and tossing them into the sky.

"Pull over," I said.

"But if we stop," my friend cautioned, "you're not going to get to meet Yakov. You still want to meet him, right?"

"Yes. . .uh, no. . .I don't know!" I stammered. "Just pull over! We can't leave this toddler in the middle of the street."

Our car glided to a stop, and I got out. The boy, suddenly aware of my presence, turned and began to walk quickly away from me. Luckily, he stepped onto the curb and walked up the sidewalk, rather than venturing deeper into traffic.

"It's okay," I said in a soothing voice. "I'm just trying to help you."

He turned onto a road that intersected the busy street where we had found him.

As I walked along beside him, my friend followed along beside us. The more I spoke to the youngster, the faster he walked.

"What's your name?" I asked.

He stared down at his grubby feet and shuffled on.

"Do you know where you live?" I asked.

Again, silence.

"How old are you?" I asked.

He extended three dirty fingers in my direction as his little feet *plop, plop, plopped* along the sidewalk.

"*Three years old?*" I thought to myself. "What kind of irresponsible parent lets a three-year-old out alone to play so close to a major thoroughfare?"

Suddenly, the little boy cut swiftly in front of me and ran up the walkway to a modest little white vinyl-sided home with gray shutters. The front door was open, and he stretched his little three-year-old body up to grasp the handle with both hands and tug open the screen door.

I stood outside of the home, confused and wondering what, if anything, I should do next. I turned to my friends sitting in the idling car. We simultaneously shrugged our shoulders at one another.

I decided to follow the boy to make certain he was all right, and to make sure that whoever was responsible for him was more conscientious in the future. I walked up the stairs and peered through the screen door. I could see the little boy standing beside a couch at the far side of a dark living room. The television set was on, and the boy had placed one hand on someone lying on the couch.

I knocked on the frame of the screen door.

No answer.

I knocked louder.

Still no answer.

"Hello?" I asked.

Nothing.

"Hello!" I shouted.

At that, a woman, who had obviously been asleep, rolled over and spoke to the child, "You okay, baby?" she asked.

"Excuse me," I said loudly. The woman, now fully awake and realizing she and the boy were not alone, rose and walked slowly over to the door. She squinted as she looked from the dark room into the sunlight.

"Yes?" she said.

"My name is Will Bowen," I said. "I just followed your little boy for more than three blocks from that major street back there. When I found him, he was alone and playing in the middle of traffic."

She stared doubtfully at me for a moment. She looked at the youngster, glanced around the room, and checked the time on the clock. Then, the realization of what had transpired leapt across her face. "Oh my God," she said.

The boy was clinging to her pant leg. She bent down and swept him up into her arms, hugging him tightly.

"Oh my God!" she repeated. "He was up the street?" Her eyes were now wide with terror.

"Yes," I said. "I found him playing in the middle of the six-lane road back there."

The full understanding of what had happened and, more significantly, what *might* have happened hit her. "I fell asleep on the couch," she said, her voice quavering. "It was warm, so I left the door open. He was watching cartoons. . .he's never done anything like this!"

She scanned her memory. "I locked the screen," she told me with certainty. Then, gazing down for a moment, she said with less conviction, "I'm *pretty sure* I locked the screen. . ."

Then she began to cry, clutching the boy to her chest.

"Oh my God!" she cried once again. She pulled the boy away and held him up in front of her, examining him for injury.

"I'm pretty sure he's okay," I said. "It's lucky that he knows where he lives. I just walked alongside him to make sure he got home safely."

"Thank you!" she shrieked, the tears flowing more heavily. "Thank you!"

"I'm glad I could help," I said.

My mind returned to its prior affirmation—"I'm going to meet Yakov"—even though my opportunity to meet him had clearly passed.

I turned to leave as the woman covered the child with kisses, but at the last moment I walked back to the doorway.

"Excuse me," I said through the screen.

"Yes?"

"What's his name?"

"Jacob," she replied, still clutching him. "His name is Jacob."

I felt a warm shudder as I walked back to the car.

Silently I put on my seat belt and settled into the seat as I replayed in my mind what had just transpired. For a week I had been anticipating meeting Yakov. For the last hour I had been affirming "I'm going to meet Yakov."

"His name is Jacob," the mother had said. In Russian, the name Jacob is pronounced as *Yakov*. My affirmation had come true.

The traffic was now moving, and we drove quickly to the show, which was under way. We managed to find seats in the back of the hall. Ahead in the front row, I could see my friend who had promised to introduce me to Yakov. She glanced over her shoulder and our eyes met.

We both smiled and she held her two hands palms up, as if to say "Oh well. Too bad." I shrugged my shoulders and nodded my head in agreement.

After the show, our group walked out into the parking lot. Something inside me told me to go back into the hall. Leaving my friends, I turned back to the auditorium. "I'll be right back," I said.

"Where are you going?" someone asked.

"I'll be back," I said again.

Just as I entered the empty venue, I ran into my friend who had offered to introduce me to Yakov. And guess who was with her? Yakov Smirnoff! Feeling it was destiny that we meet, I walked up and she introduced us.

As it turns out, Yakov and I have a lot in common—including the same birthday. We began to correspond via email and phone calls, and today he is one of my best friends. In addition to being funny, he is a sensitive, smart, and very spiritual man, committed to his own personal development and to making the world a better place for everyone.

I love this true story on so many levels. Not only did I meet and befriend Yakov, whose name would be pronounced Jacob in other languages, but I was also able to help another Jacob—a boy who might have been seriously hurt had I not been come along at just the right time to help him.

Was it my *destiny* to meet Yakov Smirnoff? Was it *fate* that I help Jacob find his way home?

Destiny Is Not Fate

Many people use the words "destiny" and "fate" interchangeably. However, their connotations are actually quite different.

Destiny is an optimal potentiality that lingers at the outer edges of our current lives. It sits quietly awaiting our approach.

Fate, on the other hand, is inevitable. Fate will occur whether we do anything to move toward it or not. Fate is something that cannot be avoided. Fate is a predetermined end, and no amount of effort can alter our arriving at its doorstep. The inevitability of fate explains where derivations of the word such as "fateful," "fatal," and "fatalistic" come from.

"Fate" is akin to "fateful." "Destiny," on the other hand, is akin to "destination." My experiences with both Yakov and Jacob were, therefore, *destiny* and not *fate*. They were the result of actions I took, rather than a predestined inevitability.

I mentioned in the introduction to this book that happiness is your destiny. It is the destination to which you are drawn; blended with the proper thoughts, words, actions, habits, and character, it is a destiny you will realize.

Many people do not fulfill their destinies—their destiny to be happy or their destiny to reach the heights of love, health, and prosperity to which they are entitled. The destinies are there; these individuals simply do not put forth the effort to reach them.

Happiness is your destiny because you and every other person have a predilection toward happiness. Embracing happiness as your aim, setting it as a goal, measuring your progress toward it, and taking steps to be a happier person brings you to your destiny.

Human beings are hardwired for happiness. This is evidenced by the fact that happiness is the standard by which life itself is measured. When someone makes a significant life change, we may make inquiries:

- *Why did you quit your job?*
- *Why did you leave your marriage?*
- *Why did you move from your hometown?*
- *Why did you change your hairstyle?*
- *Why did you stop pursuing that hobby?*

Regardless of the question, "I wasn't happy" satisfies as an answer.

"I am happy" or "I am not happy" are acceptable and complete answers to the great questions of life, underscoring that at a deep level we understand that happiness is our destiny.

Saint Augustine of Hippo felt that destiny is a merging of the soul with the body. The soul dwells in the realm of the infinite and, so, cannot understand why you don't live a life of happiness. Engaging the body in the processes that bring about a feeling of happiness fulfills your destiny to live as the happy soul that you truly are.

But—what about fate?

We are all fated to die. Death is inevitable. We are also fated to experience pain, difficulty, and tragedy in our lives. Life comes with suffering. In fact, the Buddha taught that life is suffering.

Life *is* challenging. Life *is* beset by struggle. Life *can often be* difficult. That is our fate.

And yet even saddled with the fate of living a life of challenges, our destiny can remain happiness. The venerable Vietnamese Buddhist monk Thich Nhat Hanh has written, "Don't wait until you have no more suffering before allowing yourself to be happy."

In comparing a person's destiny to one's fate, the great German philosopher Friedrich Nietzsche believed that a destiny could be fulfilled by an honest evaluation of one's fate. Understanding and embracing the thorny nature of being fated to experience challenges, and to suffer, frees us to set the destiny of becoming happier—even amidst life's ups and downs.

Many people think that if happiness is a destiny, it is one that forever looms off in the murky distance. If conditions support happiness, one is happy. If life is difficult, one is unhappy. What most people call happiness is actually a gleeful reaction to fortunate events.

Think of the ways we use the word "happy":

- *I'm happy to meet you.*
- *I was happy to discover that new restaurant.*
- *I'm happy to be with her.*
- *Congratulations on your marriage; I'm so happy for you both.*
- *I'm so happy that you called.*

Considering the frequency with how often the word happiness is thrown around, you would think that people must be a lot happier than they are. In reality, we have come to use the word "happy" when what we really mean is "pleased." More accurate statements would be:

- *I'm pleased to meet you.*
- *I was pleased to discover that new restaurant.*
- *It pleases me to be with her.*
- *Congratulations on your marriage; I'm so pleased for you both.*
- *I'm so pleased that you called.*

Being happy is a level of overall contentment, whereas *being pleased* is an expression of pleasure. We so often report being happy when, in reality, we are actually expressing a feeling of pleasure.

Pleasure comes and goes. Happiness is a general state of well-being.

Just for fun, monitor how often you use the word "happy." Then, replace it whenever possible with the word "pleased." Begin to differentiate happiness—which is based on your prevailing sense of contentment—from the fleeting experiences and people who please you.

The first step to reaching a destiny is to discover that destiny. Then to claim that it is your own. As I mentioned in Chapter 3, a belief that you are happy is the most important step toward being happy. What you believe about yourself is the key determinant of the self you will become.

Engineering Happiness authors Rakesh Sarin and Manel Baucells write that happiness is a self-fulfilling prophecy. Your destiny may be to be happy, but if you don't claim your destiny, you will never realize it. However, if you state that you *are* happy, happiness becomes a self-fulfilling prophecy.

"Is it really that important that I believe that I am happy for me to be happy?" you may be wondering. "Does what I say about myself really become a self-fulfilling prophecy?"

You Become What You Believe

A recent *Psychology Today* article reported a study conducted by the Norwegian University of Science and Technology that tested the concept of a self-fulfilling prophecy.

Researchers asked more than one thousand normal-weight teenagers how they viewed their bodies. Eleven years later, they followed up with these subjects and found that 78% of those who had reported that they considered themselves to be fat as teenagers ended up as overweight adults. The teens had declared that they were fat, even though they were not, and their obesity as adults became a self-fulfilling prophecy.

Happiness is a self-fulfilling prophecy. You'll never be any happier than you believe yourself to be.

Dostoyevsky wrote, "We are all happy if we but knew it." Whether you average a 3 on a 10-point happiness scale or an 8 on that same scale, you *are* happy, and the more you claim being happy, which kindles happiness's flames, rather than stating, "I *want* to be happy," which douses those flames, the happier you will become.

We have now come full circle. To achieve the destiny that is your destination of happiness, you must first hold a persistent thought that you are a happy person. Your thought that you are happy will direct your words and actions, building habits and developing your character.

Your destiny will remain to be happy, whether you choose to make it your pursuit or not. If you do, you can become measurably and sustainably happy this year.

RECAPPING "DESTINY OF HAPPINESS"

- You are hardwired for happiness.

- Destiny is an ideal port that you can miss if you don't intentionally sail toward it. Destiny requires your action, whereas fate is inevitable.

- Begin to save the word "happy" for use only in declaring your state of being. For things that bring you pleasure, use the word "pleased" instead.

- Remember that to "want" something means to attest to your belief that you don't have it. Cease to want to be happy. Affirm that you are happy instead.

- Happiness is a self-fulfilling prophecy. Your destiny of happiness is as close as your claiming that you have already arrived.

EPILOGUE

Imagine for a moment that it's New Year's Eve and you are sitting with friends enjoying a quiet celebration together. Music plays softly in the background as you all sit in the warm glow of candlelight. You hear the sharp pop of a champagne cork, followed by the gurgling of the wine into long-stem glasses.

As the clock slips toward midnight, someone suggests that each of you share a resolution for the coming year. After a moment of awkward silence, one of your friends proclaims, "I'm going to lose fifteen pounds."

"All right!" "Yes!" "You can do it!" and other statements of support overlay one another as glasses are raised and clinked.

Next, someone else says, "I'm going to start my own business."

Excited exclamations of approval and admiration follow, and soon, one by one, other resolutions are made, each met by toasts and enthusiastic words of encouragement.

You glance up and realize that it is nearly time for both the clock and the calendar to slip into the New Year. During a fragment of silence, you boldly declare, "I'm going to be happy!" Rather than rising to toast your resolution, the champagne glasses dip subtly as those holding them attempt to wrap their minds around what you just said.

Friendly faces attempt to smile past bewilderment, and others offer you a patronizing nod in confused and feigned support. To everyone's immense relief, the year expires at just that moment, and the singing of "Auld Lang Syne" drowns out the conversation.

Making happiness your resolution seems backward to most people. Checking off resolutions achieved makes us happy, they believe. And yet, as we've seen, happiness is not a by-product of healthy and successful living; it is the foundation upon which such a life is built.

Skyscrapers originated in America. They first became popular in the late 1800s when businessmen desired to have their entire companies close to other businesses with whom they traded. With the invention of metal I-beams, which were hundreds of times sturdier than masonry walls, skyscrapers could begin to live up to their names and truly reach the sky.

Except for one problem.

There were no elevators yet designed that could transport people to the heights to which buildings could now be built. The height of a building was not dictated by how high its internal framework could reach or how tall its outer walls could be constructed, but rather, how high its elevator could go.

In 1880, elevators could reach only 10 stories, and so that was the maximum height that buildings could be constructed. By 1890, elevators were able to reach 20 stories, and developers began to build twenty-story skyscrapers.

Over time, elevators have evolved to be able to reach higher and higher and, as a result, skyscrapers have soared.

Setting New Year's resolutions for life improvement, hoping that happiness will be the result, is like building a skyscraper that is too tall for its elevator. It may look good on the outside, but it is nothing more than a hollow edifice. However, developing happiness *first* and then pursuing external accomplishments and life improvements later, will assure that you not only reach the heights but that you will also enjoy the view from the top.

As Eckhart Tolle put it, "Be at least as interested in what goes on inside you as what happens outside. If you get the inside right, the outside will fall into place."

Here's to your happiness!